GHOST RAILROADS

A JOURNEY THROUGH YESTERYEAR

GHOST RAILROADS

OF · CENTRAL · ARIZONA

PRUETT **P** PUBLISHING COMPANY
Boulder, Colorado

JOHN · W · SAYRE

Library of Congress Cataloging in Publication Data

Sayre, John, 1954—
   Ghost railroads and ghost towns of central Arizona.

  Bibliography: p.
  Includes index.
  1. Railroads—Arizona. 2. Cities and towns, Ruined—
Arizona. 3. Arizona—History, Local.   I. Title.
TF24.A6S29   1985   979.1'5704   85-6430
ISBN: 0-87108-683-2 (pbk.)

First Edition
1 2 3 4 5 6 7 8 9

Printed in the United States of America

CONTENTS

ACKNOWLEDGEMENTS

The completion of this project was aided by the interest and assistance of several persons. First, I want to extend special thanks to Robert Krohn of Tucson and Randy Wright of Scottsdale for the excellent map and artwork that enhances this volume.

I also owe a great deal of thanks to Sue Chamberlain, the archivist of the Sharlot Hall Museum in Prescott, Arizona, for her assistance. Matt Plese and R.G. Garland of the Santa Fe Railway contributed information for which I am grateful. Linda McCleary, Kathy Ontiveros, and Carol Downing of the Arizona Department of Library, Archives and Public Records were particularly helpful. Susie Sato and the staff of the Arizona Historical Foundation also provided assistance. The aid and advice of the personnel of the Yavapai County Recorder's Office, the Yavapai County Attorney's Office, Bureau of Land Management, and Arizona Department of Mineral Resources were essential to this study.

My personal gratitude is extended to the late Blaine Bowman and Nell Nellis Goldthwaite and to Walter Goldthwaite Jr., Margaret Hallett, Mynn Jarman, Harriett Marshall, Charles Nichols, Jack Orr, David Sayre, and Charles Wolz for graciously providing photographs for this volume.

Archives that furnished photographs are the: Sharlot Hall Museum, Arizona Department of Library, Archives and Public Records, Arizona Historical Foundation, National Railway Historical Society, ALCO Photographic Collection, National Archives, University of Arizona Special Collections Library, and the Camp Verde Historical Society.

My thanks go out to Susan McDonald, David Sayre, David Moreno, Scott Ross, Fred Rozum, Judy Lohavanijaya, "the ghost," and to the many others who contributed in various ways over the past five years to the completion of this volume. I alone, however, am responsible for any errors or inadequacies that may appear in the text.

PREFACE

This manuscript is a study of the mining country south of Prescott, Arizona. It is not the one-dimensional study of the railroads, or the mines, or the ghost towns that is so common to today's bookshelves. Rather, it is the saga of how these elements had their Arizona origins, prospered and grew, and lived and died together.

We will take a brief look at the first railroads into Prescott and then study in detail the mining roads that extended south into the mineral-rich Bradshaw Mountains. We will trace the rise and demise, not just of the railroads and the mines, but also of the communities that developed along the railroad tracks. Particular attention is given to the life-style, businesses, schools, elections, and recreation of the local population. Each area has its own interesting story to tell, and these are shared in each chapter.

Last, but not least, we will take our railroad timetable and board the steam-powered train for one last journey into the mining heartland. We will see each community as it was during its peak years and discover what made it memorable.

INTRODUCTION

The ribbon of steel delivered settlers, supplies, and dreams to the American West, but just as importantly brought Eastern capital to an area wealthy in resources but desperately poor in investment. The first transcontinental railroad was completed in 1869, and by 1890 railroad tracks crisscrossed the plains and mountains of the colorful West. In that year, the Census Bureau announced that the West was officially settled, and admittedly it was a West far different from the one gazed upon by Lewis and Clark, but the area looked much more settled from offices in Washington than it did from the middle of "God's country." While Easterners availed themselves of the latest inventions and innovations, life in the West was still difficult and centered around necessities such as food, water, clothing, and shelter.

Nowhere was the rugged life-style more apparent than in mining towns. These small pockets of settlement were usually in isolated locations where chances of survival were little better than chances of striking it rich. The normal life span of mining town residents was even shorter than the national average, which, in the year 1900 was only 47.3 years. The face of mining changed as Eastern capital flowed into the mining regions of the West. Large corporations replaced prospectors and the small local mining company.

Mining in Yavapai County, Arizona Territory, experienced this transitional period in mining evolution during the decade of the eighties. Miners had worked with picks, shovels, or gold pans; valuable discoveries had made prospectors very wealthy overnight. Gold and silver discoveries attracted large numbers of miners with big hopes and small amounts of money for equipment. Until about 1890, news of each strike started a "rush."

It soon became necessary to dig deeper into the earth to recover precious and industrial metals. Mining for these metals required hundreds of feet of shafts and tunnels. These honeycombs had to be supported with timbers and ventilated by machine-driven fans. In addition, the metals deeper in the earth were very difficult to separate from worthless rock. The costly process of modern mining, smelting, and refining forced out the small local companies that were financed on a "shoestring."

The population of Yavapai County increased from 668 in 1870 to 1,759 in 1890, largely because of the growth of the mining industry. The county was rich in gold, silver, copper, lead, and zinc. More than 24,000 mining claims were filed there by May 1893, and most of these were in the Bradshaw Mountains south of Prescott. By 1890, greater than 60 percent of the county's voters were involved in mining or related occupations. Many of the men associated with the mining industry were involved in transporting and freighting ore from isolated mines to distant smelting facilities.

Numerous stage and freight routes served the mining area south of Prescott. The main north-south route from Phoenix to Prescott was the Black Canyon Stage Road. This 110-mile wagon trail skirted the foothills of the Bradshaw Mountains and journeyed through such prominent communities as New River, Tip Top, Bumble Bee, Cordes, Mayer and Massicks. Fares were eight to ten cents per mile for passengers. Other freighting companies connected Prescott with many Bradshaw Mountain mines, including ones near the settlements of Mayer, McCabe, Big Bug, Turkey Creek, Crown King, and Walker.

Freighting ore was made difficult by narrow, winding roads more suited for coyotes than ore wagons. Nevertheless, freight companies flourished, and the demand for freight teams was so great that a shortage of quality livestock existed. Draft

These teamsters are enjoying this stretch of level land, but know the travel will get more difficult when they reach the rugged terrain of mining country. *Courtesy Arizona Department of Library, Archives and Public Records.*

teams varied from four to fourteen head, depending on the size and weight of the freight. To defray their expenses, freighting companies charged "top dollar" for their services. Freight rates were so high that many shippers felt they were "held up" by the freighting companies.

The high cost of shipping ore was not the only concern of mine operators. Real holdups, ambushes, "spooked" horses, and runaway wagons claimed some ore and bullion shipments. As if those problems were not enough, Indian hostilities lingered into the seventies and disrupted freighting and mining operations. Yet another problem was the shortage of experienced mule-skinners; careless drivers caused several mishaps in the Bradshaw Mountains. Drivers and swampers and horses and mules showed great courage and generally did an admirable job, but ore shipments

were still severely limited by the enormous expense.

The region was unquestionably rich in valuable minerals. Advances in mining technology and increased demand for industrial metals made the area attractive to investors. The only ingredient that the area lacked was a means of affordable and dependable transportation. Investors and businessmen wanted a railroad built to tap the Bradshaw Mountains' wealth. The decade of the nineties witnessed fulfillment of their wish. Short freight routes still operated, but Bradshaw Mountain mines and towns prospered when they rode the rails of steel into the twentieth century.

The railroads that made expansion of the mining industry into that area possible were the Prescott and Eastern Railway and the Bradshaw Mountain Railway.

RAILROAD CONSTRUCTION

Mining in Yavapai County Began in 1863 when placer gold was discovered in Lynx Creek near present-day Prescott. News traveled quickly, and many other discoveries were made in the months that followed. The mineral-rich land south of Prescott was soon dotted with prospectors and miners filing and working claims.

The Hollywood image of the lone prospector striking out into the wilderness with little more than a pick, beans, bacon, and burro is not altogether accurate. Prospecting was a dangerous and demanding occupation, and few men set out alone. They often traveled in pairs, as the work was not only lonely but required a wealth of knowledge. The successful prospector knew a great deal about geology, geography, metallurgy, chemistry, physics, business, and law. Furthermore, he had to be rugged, part mountain goat, persistent and, above all else, lucky.

Many problems faced the mining men, but the one which proved the most difficult was the great cost to transport ore by wagon team to smelters as far away as California and Colorado. Due to the enormous cost involved in this type of transportation, only the richest ores were sent to the smelters. Many mines were not developed or left large piles of potentially profitable ore in waste dumps.

The key to the economic development of the mines near Prescott was a cheaper mode of transportation for receiving supplies and shipping ore. The solution to the dilemma was the construction of a railroad. The rail of the Atlantic and Pacific, which later became part of the Santa Fe System, crossed the northern part of Arizona in 1882. This line made the construction of a railroad

to serve Prescott and Central Arizona a step closer to reality.

The first railroad to serve Prescott was the Prescott and Arizona Central (P.& A.C. Ry.) This seventy-two mile line was built from the Atlantic and Pacific mainline near Seligman south through Chino Valley and into Prescott. The line was completed on 31 December 1886. The high hopes for the line were soon dashed by its high rates and unbusinesslike operation. The railroad owned three small locomotives, none of which was capable of pulling more than half-a-dozen cars. The line neglected for several months to build either a wye or a turntable to allow the engines to turn around; thus, they backed the entire distance on the return trip. Unfortunately, much of the rail was laid in washes and on land that was ill-suited for the right-of-way. When the rains came, many of the bridges and much of the track simply washed away. The rail was in a constant state of disrepair, as were the rolling stock and equipment in general. Timetables were not followed, and shipments were almost always late. The P. & A.C. was a disaster by 1893. The idea was rich, but the owners were not, and the road was a losing proposition. It did, however, illustrate the need for a first class railroad and made the businessmen of Prescott even more determined in their resolve to have a railroad in their mile high city.

Frank M. Murphy, a Prescott businessman whose name is almost synonymous with Central Arizona railroading, began efforts in the late 1880s to have another railroad built to Prescott. His plan, which called for the construction of a railroad from the Atlantic and Pacific mainline near Ash Fork

Frank M. Murphy, the father of railroading in Yavapai County and Central Arizona. *Courtesy Sharlot Hall Museum.*

south to Prescott, was originally to have been financed, in large part, by "Diamond" Joe Reynolds. Reynolds, a mining mogul and owner of the rich Congress Mine north of Wickenburg, died before the plans could be completed. His estate contributed heavily to Murphy's project, but increased funding was needed to finance construction of the railroad. Murphy, a man of great determination, continued to lay the groundwork for the project and sought additional investors.

He was a man of great imagination, insight, and business acumen, but perhaps more importantly was an exceptional salesman and promoter. He contacted his wealthy and influential uncle, Simon Murphy of Chicago, and succeeded in interesting him in his railroad venture. Simon Murphy's associates, Marshall Field of department store fame and Dexter Ferry of the mail order seed business, were so impressed with Frank Murphy and his plan that they also invested in the railroad.

Frank Murphy took his plans to the Arizona Territorial Legislature in 1891 hoping to receive aid in the form of tax exempt status for the railroad. The legislature strongly supported Murphy's plan and on 16 March 1891 passed a bill which granted twenty years of tax exempt status to Arizona Territory railroads, which began construction within six months. The last stumbling block cleared, Murphy and his financial supporters incorporated the Santa Fe, Prescott and Phoenix Railway Company (S.F., P. & P. Ry.) on 27 May 1891. The Atchison, Topeka and Santa Fe Railway Company (A.T.&S.F. Ry.) also invested heavily in Murphy's railroad venture. In exchange for an

The Santa Fe, Prescott and Phoenix Railway was nicknamed the Pea Vine for the number of steep, twisting curves along its mainline. This photograph shows several trestles and the winding rail north of Prescott. *Courtesy National Archives 48-RST-3A-11.*

Santa Fe, Prescott and Phoenix Railway locomotive No. 1, with combination-coach in tow, awaits passengers at the Ash Fork Depot for its run south through Prescott and Phoenix. *Courtesy Arizona Historical Foundation, Hayden Library, Arizona State University.*

equal value of stock in the new company, the A.T. & S.F. Ry. supplied $20,000 worth of second-hand rail to the young railroad. The standard gauge rail was planned to connect with the Santa Fe mainline near Ash Fork, travel south to Prescott, then southwest past the Congress Mine and eastward to Phoenix.

Skilled crews were quickly assembled, and work started south from Ash Fork. The construction of long winding trestles slowed progress as several deep canyons were crossed. At times, the rail inched forward at little more than a snail's pace. All obstacles overcome, the S.F., P. & P. Ry. arrived in Prescott in April 1893. The Pea Vine, as this line was affectionately called due to its many twisting curves and steep challenging grades, reached its Phoenix terminus in March 1895. The rail effectively linked Prescott and Phoenix with the refinements of the East and West by the Santa Fe mainline.

The Pea Vine was met with great enthusiasm in Prescott. The population increased dramatically and was near 3,600 by the turn of the century. The quality of life also improved. Refinements from the East, cultural, social, and financial, found their way to Prescott. Merchants quickly established themselves, and the service sector expanded to meet the needs of the growing little town. The most important cargo the railroad brought to Prescott during these early days was the capitalists and financiers of the East.

The rich mines south of Prescott were desperately in need of capital which just wasn't available locally. The railroad made expansion and development of the mining industry profitable through reduced transportation costs. Eastern capitalists poured money into the Bradshaw Mountains south of Prescott. The romantic metals, gold and silver, drew a great deal of money to the area, but the growing market for copper brought unexpectedly large-scale investment.

Investors soon clamored for a railroad to be built from Prescott into the Bradshaw Mountains. What they actually wanted was for Murphy to invest in the railroad so they could invest in mining, as few men ever found the "mother lode" in the cab of a railroad locomotive. This new railroad was surveyed from Prescott to serve the mines in the Agua Fria Valley and the heartland of the southern Bradshaw Range. Murphy, maps in hand, made another trip to the Midwest and talked with "Uncle Simon" and his friends. He returned from Chicago with the financial backing once again of Simon

7

The old Santa Fe, Prescott and Phoenix Railway Depot at Phoenix, the southern terminus of the Pea Vine, is pictured here circa 1900. *Courtesy Arizona Department of Library, Archives and Public Records.*

Murphy and Dexter Ferry. He also managed to secure the support of capitalists C.C. Bowen, N.K. Fairbank, Jay Morton, and G.W. Kretzinger. He approached the Territory of Arizona early in 1897 and, as he had done in 1891, requested favored tax status for his proposed railroad. The Nineteenth Territorial Legislature passed a bill on 16 March 1897 that tax exempted new railroads for fifteen years if they incorporated within six months of the bill's passage. The new railroad, named the Prescott and Eastern (P.& E.), was legally born on 14 September 1897. The road was planned to connect with the Pea Vine just north of majestic Granite Dells and be twenty-six miles in length, having its terminus near the Black Canyon Stage station of Joe Mayer.

Only a few years earlier, Granite Dells, or Point of Rocks as it was sometimes called, was one of the most feared locations in the Territory. Mail carriers and stage teamsters were easy targets when traveling the road through the Dells. The large boulders and outcroppings were excellent hiding places from which renegade Indians attacked travelers and settlers. In the 1870s, the Indian hostilities diminished, but the Dells continued to draw lawbreakers. Gunfire still echoed off the granite landscape into the eighties, as the terrain provided good cover for highwaymen and local

desperados. Law and order finally took hold by the 1890s, however, and the locomotives, unlike the old stages, did not need anyone "riding' shotgun."

Murphy contacted several construction companies with the specifications of the Prescott and Eastern road and advertised for bids on the project. Contractors were given until February 1898 to submit their bids to Murphy at the offices of the S.F., P.&P.Ry. in Prescott. The bids were opened in Late February, and the contract was awarded to the Montana and Arizona Construction Company. The President of this firm, Donald Grant, had his men grading by 1 March and working under full headway by the tenth of the month.

The contractors quickly established two construction camps, from which operations were coordinated. The first was just north of Granite Dells where the P. & E. left the S.F., P.&P.Ry. line, and the other camp was about two miles farther along the proposed route. Seventy men were employed doing rock work at the camp near the junction with the Pea Vine, and thiι:y-three men and twenty-seven wagon teams were doing grading work out of the second camp. The construction crews grew to 350 men as the contractor geared up to meet the six month construction deadline specified in his contract.

The railroad construction foremen constantly

8

fought a shortage of manpower. At times the shortages became so severe that the Yavapai County Sheriff became an employment counselor of sorts. Hobos, transients, and others among the unemployed were arrested for vagrancy and thrown in jail. The advantages of working for steady wages instead of sitting behind bars were then pointed out by sheriff's personnel. Many of the petty criminals were released to join the railroad construction crews. The work didn't require a diploma, resume, or experience.

The work was primarily completed by hand. Pick and shovel work was the method of the day. Rudimentary scrapers and leveling devices attached to wagons and drawn by powerful teams sped progress and made the physically demanding jobs bearable. Working on a railroad construction crew was not a job for the weak of body. The work was long, backbreaking, and, as might be expected, didn't pay well. The men that worked on these crews south of Prescott were primarily Greeks, Italians, and "vagrants." The Greeks and Italians were brought to the area specifically for the construction of this railroad line, and most left the area after the line was completed. A few Mexicans and Indians also worked on this line but comprised only a small portion of the work force. The Chinese, who worked very effectively on railroad construction crews elsewhere, were not used on the Prescott and Easter.

The spring was a mild one, and the favorable weather conditions allowed crews to grade 12 miles of roadbed by May 1898. As the smell of spring and wildflowers filled the air, concern was voiced over a shortage of rail. Only about two miles of rail had been laid, and this was only used to receive supplies from the Pea Vine. Shipments of rail finally started arriving on schedule, and crews hurried to make up lost time. Progress remained steady over the summer, but the grading work became more difficult and extensive; some areas required up to eighteen feet of fill. Almost twenty miles of roadbed were completed and track laid by late July. Work continued frantically on the remaining six miles of roadbed as summer drew to a close. Although a great deal of construction work remained to be completed on railroad buildings and loading platforms, the rail reached its terminus at Mayer on schedule. While the autumn leaves fell crimson and gold, the train chugged into Mayer. The first scheduled run was made on 15 October 1898.

The Prescott and Eastern was a relatively short railroad but crossed a diversity of beautiful countryside. The first two miles of the line from the P. & E. Junction passed through the scenic granite landscape of Granite Dells. The rail then passed through Lonesome Valley and on to a siding established near the road to Jerome. This siding was named Yaeger after the canyon of that name. The line then crossed Lynx Creek and descended into the lush grain fields of the Agua Fria Valley. Near the old Hildebrandt Ranch in the upper Agua Fria Valley, the first depot on the line, Cherry Creek, was established. At the Bowers' Ranch, near present-day Humboldt, the P. & E. veered southwest toward the Bradshaw foothills and the mineral-laden Big Bug country. As the roadbed ascended from the Agua Fria Valley, it followed Big Bug Creek past the depot at Huron and on to the terminus at Mayer. The peaks of the Bradshaw Mountains peered through wispy clouds and were visible from the depot in Mayer. They beckoned the rail onward.

The Prescott and Eastern's contribution to the development of Yavapai County cannot be overstated. It gave direction and impetus to the development of the mining industry in the area south of Prescott. The rail brought in almost as much Eastern capital as it shipped out ore. The mineral deposits in the area were vast and spread out southwest like a large fan from Jerome. The P. & E. delivered shipments of heavy equipment and mining machinery to hundreds of Bradshaw Mountain mines. A large mill and smelter were constructed near Bowers' Ranch on the Agua Fria River. The sound of stamp mills, gasoline powered hoists, and general construction soon filled the Bradshaw Range as mining operations expanded. The P. & E. didn't transport just mining supplies and ore. The number of passengers and amount of personal freight carried on the line were substantial at the turn of the century.

Mayer and Huron rapidly became distribution points for the southern Bradshaw area and the Agua Fria Valley. The town of Mayer, which prior to the arrival of the P. & E. was little more than a stage station on the Black Canyon Stage Route, was suddenly the center of economic and population growth. Carpenters and masons built a variety of buildings that accommodated the sudden growth in population and the new business sector. Conditions in Huron and Humboldt were much the same, and construction was going on virtually everywhere along the line. The early freight shipments to these communities were high in commodities other than mining supplies. This indicates that the railroad met a need for items to improve the quality of life. The business sectors grew rapidly to meet the varied needs of the increased population.

The P. & E. also carried large shipments of livestock, primarily sheep, from the area around Mayer. Mayer was on the sheep trail between Flagstaff, where the sheep spent the summer, and

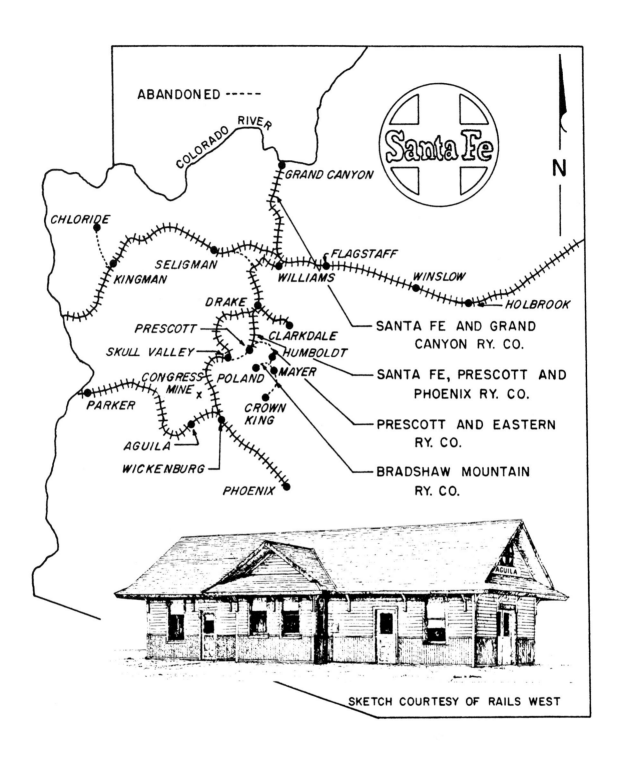

ABANDONED - - - - -

COLORADO RIVER

GRAND CANYON

Santa Fe

N

CHLORIDE

SELIGMAN
KINGMAN

FLAGSTAFF

WILLIAMS

WINSLOW

HOLBROOK

DRAKE

SANTA FE AND GRAND
CANYON RY. CO.

PRESCOTT

CLARKDALE

HUMBOLDT

SANTA FE, PRESCOTT AND
PHOENIX RY. CO.

SKULL VALLEY

MAYER

POLAND

CONGRESS
MINE x

PRESCOTT AND EASTERN
RY. CO.

PARKER

CROWN
KING

BRADSHAW MOUNTAIN
RY. CO.

AGUILA

WICKENBURG

PHOENIX

AGUILA

SKETCH COURTESY OF RAILS WEST

THE PRINCIPAL LINES OF THE
SANTA FE RAILWAY SYSTEM IN ARIZONA

MAP BY ROB KROHN

Phoenix, where they were driven for the winter. In the spring months, the P. & E. railhead at Mayer served as the shipping point for thousands of sheep to the meat packing center of Chicago.

The great success of the Prescott and Eastern was the talk of Central Arizona. Thousands of mines dotted the countryside to the west and southwest of Mayer. Shipments of ore and mining supplies were heavy and so encouraging that Frank Murphy thought about expanding the P. & E. into the heart of the mining country.

Murphy approached the financial backers of the P. & E. with the idea of building branch lines into the rugged terrain of the Bradshaws. Their response was favorable, and Murphy incorporated the Bradshaw Mountain Railway (B.M. Ry.) on 6 February 1901. The railroad had two branches from the P. & E.; one to serve the rich Big Bug Mining District and the other the Peck, Tiger, and Pine Grove Districts to the south. Murphy approached the Territorial Legislature with hopes of a tax break for this railroad also. As in the past, the legislature passed a tax exempt status bill with Murphy in mind. The railroads that benefitted were those within the Arizona Territory that filed intent-to-build documents within a six month filing deadline. The period of exemption was ten years, and this act became law on 20 February 1901 when Territorial Governor Nathan O. Murphy, Frank Murphy's brother, signed the bill.

The Bradshaw Mountain Railroad was incorporated with capital stock of $1,050,000; however, this figure was increased in November 1905 to $2,500,000. The railroad constructed two branches as originally proposed. The Poland Branch left the P. & E. about one mile south of Huron and followed Big Bug Creek for almost eight miles to the rich Poland Mine. The other line, the Crown King Branch, was built from the Prescott and Eastern terminus in Mayer to the Crown King Mine in the pine-covered slopes of the higher Bradshaws. This 28 mile ribbon of steel was very costly to construct, as it traversed some of the most breathtaking and treacherous country in the Southwest.

The rail for the Bradshaw Mountain Branch came from the Rock Butte section of the S.F., P. & P. Ry. That section of track had been abandoned in 1901 when the Pea Vine mainline was rerouted over the Hell Canyon Cutoff. The rail was torn up and moved to Mayer, where it was stockpiled, along with ties, and awaited completion of the grade.

Progress on the Poland Branch of the railroad was rapid as right-of-way was obtained, construction crews assembled, and grading begun. The Grant Brothers contracting firm, under the supervision of Donald Grant, did the grading work for this branch. The experienced Grant, whom it

may be remembered supervised similar work for the P. & E. four years earlier, had his abilities taxed by the challenging Poland Branch. The terrain was considerably more rugged, which made the work difficult. The landscape became rocky and mountainous a short distance west of the P. & E. mainline at Poland Junction. In addition to the normal scraping and pickax work, considerable amounts of drilling and blasting were necessary on the right-of-way.

The railroad crews encountered many foreseen adversities, including the construction of terraced roadbed, two trestles, the shortest of which was 100 feet in length, and a tunnel nearly 200 feet long through solid rock. They also encountered a quite unexpected problem. In January 1902, while grading the roadbed about four miles west of the junction, the workers discovered gold. They uncovered a body of ore eight feet wide and 400 feet long. The ore, which was valued at more than $30 per ton, created a considerable commotion. The owners of the property were quick to arrive and demand that their ore be piled neatly off to the side and not be used for grading purposes. The laborers, crazed by the experience, had thoughts of uncovering an "El Dorado" of their own. Why should they do backbreaking labor for two dollars a day when the land was so rich that gold lay only a few feet below the surface?

Amid the chaos, the contractor tried to restore order and maintain a work force on the project. Many of the workers left the crew to prospect for other discoveries. Few of these men made discoveries, as those knowledgeable about prospecting or mining weren't working on the railroad in the first place. In March 1902, two railroad carloads of Italian laborers were imported from the Midwest to supplement the construction crews. The railroad employed large numbers of Greek and Italian stonemasons, as they were valued for their skill in building smooth, mortarless retaining walls along the right-of-way.

The first of the two stations on the Poland Branch was located at Providence about four and one-half miles west of the junction with the P. & E. The 125 men who were employed laying steel and the 25 men who constructed bridges finished the rail to Providence in early April 1902. The celebration that followed lasted only one day, but reportedly was so intense that many crew members could not resume work for several days. As the work on the line proceeded, the owners of property near the Poland Mine were busy laying out a townsite, building houses for miners and merchants, and establishing water and electrical systems. The rail reached Poland on 21 April 1902, and the father of the road, Frank M. Murphy, rode

This is not the Poland Tunnel, as often erroneously reported, but is the tunnel on the Poland Branch of the Bradshaw Mountain Railway. *Courtesy Sharlot Hall Museum.*

the rail to the branch terminus. The first regularly scheduled train over the line to the depot, christened Poland, rolled into the new community on 11 May 1902. Emphasis now focused on completing the Crown King Branch, which was already in progress.

Work on the first few miles of the Crown King Branch went well. With the exception of the arduous three mile stretch of Cedar Canyon, the landscape was relatively level and forgiving. The line left Mayer, cut through Cedar Canyon, and crossed the ranching country west of Cordes Station on the Black Canyon Stage Route before heading south toward Crazy Basin. The Grant Brothers Railroad Construction Company also had the contract for the grading work on this branch of the Bradshaw Mountain Railway. They had twelve miles of rail laid out of Mayer by 8 January 1903 and were nearing the powerhouse of George Middleton in Crazy Basin.

The first of the two depots on the Crown King Branch, named Middelton, was established near the Middleton powerhouse in Crazy Basin. George Middleton spelled his name with an "le," while the railroad, for some reason, spelled Middelton with an "el." A construction camp was also established at the location to serve the large crews needed to push the rail over the summit and into Crown King,

perched high on the slopes above the 6,000 feet level. As many as 600 men were employed to complete the next few miles of road, which many thought impossible to build. Middelton was also the site of a temporary turntable constructed to allow the engines to turn around before heading back down the line to Mayer. Although supply trains reached Middelton as early as January 1903, the first scheduled train did not reach the small community until 7 June of that year.

The remaining thirteen miles of rail to Crown King were considered by some to be an engineering feat and by others to be a Bradshaw boondoggle. To reach the Crown King Mine from Middelton, a series of tall ridges had to be crossed. These geographic features rose nearly 2,000 feet above Crazy Basin and proved to be challenging not only from an engineering perspective, but in financial terms as well. The ascent began at Middelton, where the first ten switchbacks was located. The distance from Middelton to the top of the "summit," as the plateau on the final ridge was called, was only two miles, but the terrain necessitated seven miles of rail to cover the distance. Much of the rail was laid at a difficult 4 percent grade. The great difficulty of construction and enormous cost of this part of the line were vastly underestimated by Murphy and his men.

This construction crew is hard at work laying the rail of the Prescott and Eastern Railway through Lonesome Valley.
Courtesy National Archives 92-F-79B-21.

The summit was finally reached in late October 1903, and the railroad proudly ran a special excursion train to the location on 17 November of that year to showcase its engineering masterpiece.

The panoramic view from the summit was a highlight for passengers on the Crown King Branch. The steep climb from Crazy Basin seemed to lead upward into the sky. The visual grandeur was inspiring as white, cottonball clouds hung so low over the summit that they could almost be touched. Scenic beauty as far away as fifty miles was visible from the lofty lookout point.

The rail was still six miles from Crown King, but the worst terrain was behind the construction crews. The next nemesis proved to be the weather. Snow dusted the mountains much earlier and heavier than expected. The harsh winter plagued the work crews as they fought blizzards and intense cold. The wake of winter soon enveloped the high country in snowy stillness. The line to Crown King was completed in the spring after the warm rays of the sun chased the snow from the ground. Regular travel to the Crown King depot began in mid-May 1904. The Bradshaw Mountain Railway, which extended sixty miles out of Prescott, was now officially completed.

RAIL OF THE PRESCOTT & EASTERN RY. AND BRADSHAW MOUNTAIN RY. THROUGH CENTRAL ARIZONA

SCALE: 1"= 6 MILES

MAP BY ROB KROHN

14

RAILROAD OPERATION

The railroad successfully reached the heartland of the rich Bradshaw Mountain mining districts, and ore production figures show the railroad's impact. Production statistics for the Big Bug District, which was served by the Poland Branch Line, increased substantially. In the year 1901, prior to the arrival of the railroad, only 11,580 tons of crude ore valued at $295,613 were mined in the district. These figures reached yearly totals of 68,577 tons and $837,510 by 1907. The Crown King Branch Line had a similar impact. The Peck District near Middelton reported production of 15 tons of ore in 1904 valued at $83. The figures in 1907 showed 23,571 tons mined with a value of $213,506.

The combined production statistics of the Tiger and Pine Grove Districts near Crown King showed figures of 5,430 tons and $85,305 in 1904. The first full year of rail service by the Bradshaw Mountain Railway increased these figures to 31,796 tons and $339,166 in 1905. It should be noted, however, that figures for the first year of rail service were deceptively large, as ore was stockpiled awaiting the arrival of the railroad. The Tiger and Pine Grove Districts' production figures for 1907, which are more representative of the districts' true growth, were 8,097 tons and $108,605. The impressive early figures and shipping receipts created a false sense of prosperity for the railroad. Large shipments of machinery and equipment were made into the mountains, but ore shipments, excluding the ore that was stockpiled, were disappointing. Nevertheless, the railroad was busy carrying ore and supplies; everyone felt that it was just a matter of time until mining production reached new peak levels.

The early success of these railroads prompted requests from mining men for more routes into the mining districts. Among the proposals given serious consideration were rail lines from Crown King to Oro Belle, Turkey Creek to points south, Huron to McCabe, and Humboldt to Stoddard. Surveys were made, but economic conditions put an end to plans real or imagined for other standard gauge feeder routes south of Prescott. Talk of such routes was revived from time to time over the next several years, but little more than conversation, resulted.

That the railroad stimulated and increased production in the districts is obvious, but the area grew in much broader terms than mineral production. To develop the mines and increase production, more miners were needed. When they arrived, they needed food, housing, and other essentials. Carpenters and merchants arrived to meet the needs of the small camps and towns. Saloons, barber shops, restaurants, and boardinghouses soon flourished near the areas of great mining activity. The rapidly growing service sector greatly improved the quality of life in the area. The histories of the different communities vary, but one common factor was the stimulus the railroad provided to their economic and population growth.

In some cases, the small towns were actually created by the railroad as it constructed numerous buildings and structures to serve its line. Depots were built at Cherry Creek (Dewey), Humboldt, Huron, and Mayer on the Prescott and Eastern Line, and at Providence, Poland, Middelton, and Crown King on the Bradshaw Mountain Lines. In these communities, the railway company constructed houses for its agents that manned the depots. Water tanks were built near the depots in Humboldt, Mayer, Providence, Middelton, and Crown King. Dormitory style housing was built at P. & E. Junction, Humboldt, Mayer, Poland,

Middelton, and Crown King for the laborers and foremen who maintained the rail, ties, trestles, and other railroad property. Numerous warehouses, tool houses, loading platforms, and other structures were also constructed along the lines.

Several sidings and spurs were laid at various points to serve the different mines and camps along the line. These included spurs or sidings at Yaeger, Chaparral, Poland Junction, and Arizona City on the Prescott and Eastern; Henrietta, Eugenie, and Block on the Poland Branch; and Gray Eagle, Blue Bell, Cordes, Turkey Creek, Peck, Saddle, and Horse Thief on the Crown King Branch. The rail at these locations varied in length from the 106-car capacity yard at Humboldt to two-car capacity flagstops. The yard at Humboldt was by far the largest on the line as the smelter in that community received ore from hundreds of mines throughout Central Arizona. The next largest yards were in Mayer, Crown King, and the "new" Henrietta Spur. Many of the sidetracks held 15-20 cars, which proved adequate for the mines of the area. Even the short spurs witnessed considerable activity as they made the operation of small local mines profitable.

The Santa Fe, Prescott and Phoenix Railway, Prescott and Eastern Railway, and Bradshaw Mountain Railway were legally independent roads but were owned and controlled by the same interests. Stock ownership of the P. & E. and B.M. Ry. was held by the S.F., P. & P. Ry. The two smaller companies did not own any railroad cars of their own and used the rolling stock of the S.F., P. & P. As might be expected, much of the rolling stock used on the railroads was the hopper bottom ore cars and boxcars; however, livestock cars, flat cars, and tankers joined the coaches and combination-coaches on the winding ribbon of steel through the Bradshaw Mountains. The trains of both mountain railroads ran out of the S.F., P. & P. yard in Prescott.

Locomotives were also supplied by the Pea Vine. When that line began service in 1893, it did so with six engines. It added two more in 1894, another in 1895, three more in 1898, and when three more were received in 1903, the total number in operation on, or in the control of, the S.F., P. & P. Ry. was brought to fifteen. Engine numbers 1 through 9 were lettered for the S.F., P. & P., numbers 10 through 12 were lettered for the P. & E., the superstitious number 13 was omitted, and locomotives 14 through 16 were lettered for the Arizona and California Railway, another subsidiary of the Pea Vine.

The three engines of the P. & E., which arrived in

Prescott and Eastern locomotive No. 11 as she looked in 1898. *Courtesy ALCO Photographs.*

This photograph of the Santa Fe, Prescott and Phoenix Railway's "lucky seven spot" was taken in 1894. The engine saw a great deal of activity on the Poland Branch of the Bradshaw Mountain Railway. The little engine remained in service on the rail of the Santa Fe System until 1931 when she was scrapped. *Courtesy ALCO Photographs.*

1898, were improved mechanically over the models already in use by the S.F., P. & P. Ry. They utilized electric headlights instead of the old kerosene lamp design. The new headlights used a generator located in front of and near the smokestack to produce a 1600 candlepower light beam and cast it more than a mile up the rail. Operations in poor weather and after nightfall were greatly enhanced by the new light source.

With only three engines the P. & E. was unable to handle the early volume of ore shipments on the Poland Branch Line. The hardworking engines were joined by the "lucky seven spot" and locomotives numbers 8 and 9 of the S.F., P. & P. in providing the motive power for the mining railroad. All six locomotives regularly used on the line were 4-6-0 wheel-patterned coal-burners built by the Brooks Locomotive Company. Shortly after the turn of the century, the locomotives were converted to burn oil. The shift in fuel was directed at alleviating the cinder-fire problems that plagued all coal-burning engines and was made possible by the growth of the refining industry on the West Coast.

Motive power on the Crown King Line presented problems uniquely its own. The engines of the S.F., P. & P. made the steep haul up to Crown King during construction and when the line first opened, but the small engines were not designed to handle the brutal 4 percent grades. In May 1904, the Bradshaw Mountain Railway ordered three engines from the American Locomotive Company to use on the challenging new line. These engines were 2-8-0 wheel-patterned, consolidation-type, oil-burning locomotives. These engines, which were small by later steam standards, carried 2,500 gallons of oil and nearly 5,500 gallons of water. As shipments increased, an order was placed for three more of the engines in 1906. The six locomotives were lettered for the B.M. Ry. and were numbered 51 through 56. These engines were the workhorses of the mountain railroad and remained in use on the Santa Fe System until they were scrapped in the forties.

The lettering and numbering of the locomotives were changed several times over the years as the Santa Fe, Prescott and Phoenix Railway and the two smaller lines were absorbed into the Santa Fe

STEAM LOCOMOTIVES REGULARLY USED IN THE BRADSHAW MOUNTAINS

RAILWAY COMPANY FOR WHICH THE LOCOMOTIVE WAS LETTERED AND NUMBERED	ENGINE NUMBER	YEAR BUILT	MANUFACTURER	WHEEL PATTERN	YEAR SCRAPPED
Santa Fe, Prescott & Phoenix Ry.	7	1894	Brooks Locomotive Co.	4-6-0	1931
	8	1894	"	"	1927
	9	1895	"	"	1922
Prescott and Eastern Ry.	10	1898	"	"	1922
	11	1898	"	"	1927
	12	1898	"	"	1922
Bradshaw Mountain Ry.	51	1904	American Locomotive Co.	2-8-0	1940
	52	1904	"	"	1951
	53	1904	"	"	1947
	54	1906	"	"	Unknown, but presumably in the 1940s
	55	1906	"	"	1940
	56	1906	"	"	1939

Note: S.F., P. & P. engines Nos. 5 and 6 were occasionally pressed into service on the Poland Branch Line, but saw most of their activity on the Pea Vine mainline.

Bradshaw Mountain Railway locomotive No. 53 stands proudly outside the American Locomotive Company factory. The engine was just completed and lettered for the mountain railway. *Courtesy Blaine Bowman.*

The American Locomotive Company delivered shiny, new engine No. 56 to the S.F., P. & P. Ry. in 1906. The 2-8-0, consolidation-type, oil-burner was originally lettered for another subsidiary of the Pea Vine, the Arizona and California Railway (A. & C.). Upon its arrival in Prescott, however, the locomotive was assigned to the Bradshaw Mountain Railway and lettered for that company. *Courtesy ALCO Photographs.*

System. The Santa Fe System had obtained controlling interest in the S.F., P. & P. from Murphy in 1901 and thereby also gained control of the Prescott and Eastern Line. The expensive Bradshaw Mountain Railway was constructed with considerable financial assistance from the Santa Fe System, which controlled the line from its inception.

Due to the favored tax status under which these railroads were incorporated, the Santa Fe System operated them as legally independent roads. When the tax exemptions expired in 1911 and 1912, the railroads were sold to the California, Arizona and Santa Fe Railway Company. This company subsequently leased the roads to the Atchison, Topeka and Santa Fe. The corporate maneuvering aside the reorganization was primarily on paper. The Atchison, Topeka and Santa Fe System had controlled the lines for years, and with the exception of locomotive lettering, little change was seen along the rail.

The trains of these mountain roads often consisted of the locomotive, two or three ore cars, a combination-coach that carried baggage and passengers, and a couple of boxcars. This equipment was manned by the engineer, fireman, conductor, flagman, brakeman, and rear brakeman. Locomotives were "doubled up," meaning that two were used, if the load or track conditions warranted. On special occasions, the railroad ran excursion trains over the route. These were usually run on holidays like the Fourth of July, at the request of Prescott merchants, or to celebrate some railroad event. These popular excursion trains were usually two or three passenger cars long and were packed with the local population. Special tickets and fares were also available from the railroad for hunters interested in taking the train to good hunting areas, for sightseers wishing to visit the Grand Canyon, and for army veterans traveling to their yearly reunions.

The railroad provided many services to towns along its tracks. Of course, large shipments of ore were made which enabled mines to employ many men but other shipments were also important to residents served by the line. The railroad delivered ice for iceboxes, coal for stoves, fresh meat and fruit, medicine from pharmacies in Prescott, and even mail-order merchandise from faraway cities. Virtually everything from pianos to chicken wire found its way onto the mountain railroads at one time or another. News and mail also arrived via the railroad, and mail days always carried a sense of excitement.

The railroad delivered mail bags to postal clerks at small post offices in communities along the line. Another service provided by these mining railroads was the operation of a railroad post office (R.P.O.).

This was a small office which operated out of the car in which the mail was carried. Railroad post office clerks directly handled only a small portion of all the mail sent, as their prime purpose was to deliver the bags of mail to established post offices. They did, however, hand cancel mail that was posted at a station or R.P.O. car, sent special delivery or registered mail, or left with a station agent for mailing. The residents of whistle stops without any other mail service welcomed the service heartily.

The railroads ran daily during the first few years when the mining industry was healthy and ore shipments were large. However, as the road was primarily a mining road, its fortunes lay with the metals market. Several up-and-down periods were encountered and weathered by the railroads over the years of operation. Railroad revenue depended not only on local mine development and operations but upon the condition of the national economy and world-wide metals market as well. It was a world-wide calamity, World War I, that provided a resurgence to the sagging fortunes of the railroads in Central Arizona. The majority of the rich mines so plentiful at the turn of the century were worked out and closed by 1911. The few that remained open did not merit daily trains and only received service three days each week.

The outbreak of hostilities on the European continent created a great demand for copper and other strategic military metals. Price supports and other governmental subsidies prompted the reopening and re-evaluation of many Bradshaw Mountain mines. Ore production was pushed to meet the enormous demand. Mineral production and railroad traffic reached unprecedented levels early in 1916. Throughout 1916 and 1917, the black smoke and shrill whistle of locomotives pulling ore cars were constant sights and sounds in the Bradshaw range. The smelter at Humboldt was working at maximum capacity, and in July 1917 the railroad yard there handled almost 600 cars of freight, mostly ore shipments.

Unfortunately for the mining and railroad industries of Yavapai County, when the European bloodshed ended, the metals market dried up. A glut flooded the world metals market, price supports were discontinued, and the price paid for non-precious metals plummeted. Just as suddenly as prosperity had returned to the mining roads, it departed. Mines closed, the smelter shut down, and miners and merchants moved elsewhere in search of employment. The railway was forced to lay off many of its workers, and equipment fell into disuse and disrepair.

Although better highways, improved heavy duty trucks, and a costly wage package won by the railroad workers' union devastated the railroads nationally, these factors had little to do with the demise of the mining roads into the Bradshaws. These lines were *mining railroads* and relied almost exclusively on ore and equipment shipments for revenue. The real problem was the lack of dependable substantial shippers along the lines. The abandonment of some mines and the closure of others killed the P. & E. and the B.M. Ry.

The ties lay rotting in the early twenties, and the trestles spanning deep canyons took on the appearance of a ghost railroad. The unpainted and forlorn buildings were vacant, and deterioration of the tracks rapidly made operation of the line unsafe. Shipping rate reductions and other incentives offered by the railroad could not combat the abandonment of mining properties and the depressed metals market. The rail retreated from the Bradshaw Mountains in segments. The first segment removed was the unprofitable, but spectacular section of track from Middelton to Crown King. The railroad ran a special excursion train in the fall of 1926 to allow the friends of the railroad and Crown King to say farewell to that part of the countryside. The Sunday afternoon train was full of passengers, stories, and tears as it pulled away from the Crown King depot for the last time. That portion of the line was officially abandoned on 14 November 1926, only two decades after it was constructed.

Many more abandonments followed. The Poland Branch Line, which was reconditioned in the mid-twenties after it became dangerously unsafe, was the next line abandoned. Most of the line—Poland to Henrietta, a distance of six miles—was abandoned and removed 10 November 1932. The Crown King Branch retreated to Cordes Siding in December 1932 and farther to the Blue Bell Siding near Mayer on 25 December 1939. The abandonment of the Poland Branch was completed back to Poland Junction on 10 April 1939. The ties were sold to ranchers for fence posts, and the rail was sold for scrap. After the rail and ties were removed, the railroad grades were used as auto roads. The abandoned railroad trestles were covered with planking and used as temporary bridges. The county felt these trestles were unsafe and eventually had them torn down and the roads rerouted around the canyons.

Several miles of the roads to Crown King and the site where Poland once stood are still built upon the railroad grades. From the dirt roadway, the caved tunnel of the Poland Branch as well as the canyons where the trestles once stood can be seen. Traveling the switchbacks up to the summit near Crown King is still a white knuckle ride even in modern vehicles, and the view is still truly

The last train over the railway to Crown King carried passengers, stories, and tears as it pulled away from the Crown King Depot for the final time. *Courtesy Mynne Jarman.*

outstanding. The railroad grade of the old P. & E. is still visible in many places as it parallels state highway 69 for much of the distance from Mayer to Dewey.

Service continued to the Blue Bell Siding near Mayer until 1958, when the rail withdrew to the Iron King Spur near Humboldt. The last section of the old Prescott and Eastern Railway, from near Humboldt to P. & E. Junction near Granite Dells, was abandoned and torn up with little fanfare in 1974. The line was always a mining road and served the Iron King until that mine shut down in the late 1960s. The line simply wasn't paying for itself, and the Santa Fe System, hard hit by the economy, could not justify operation of the line. The little railroad faded into the past.

Operation of the Prescott and Eastern and the Bradshaw Mountain Railways was handled in a very business-like and professional manner. Equipment was well-maintained and kept in safe operating condition, timetables were strictly adhered to, and employees were skilled, courteous, dedicated, and well-trained. Minor accidents occurred on the roads but were generally nothing more than derailments and an occasional overturned car. Safety on the line was enhanced by the cautious speed at which the trains were operated and the lack of congestion on the line. Delays in service, which were not common, usually involved minor derailments or track damage caused by heavy rains. The cars were maneuvered back onto the track, or the track was repaired and service quickly restored. Livestock on the open range contributed to many of the minor accidents as the cattle roamed along the tracks and were large enough to derail a car or even the engine if hit. Ranchers and the railroad alleviated this problem to a large extent by fencing the right-of-way in many areas. Everyone associated with the mountain railroads was proud of their contribution to the development of Central Arizona.

During the first years of operation, the Prescott and Eastern Railway and the Bradshaw Mountain Railway experimented with various timetables and points of departure for their trains. Prior to the completion of the Poland Branch Line, a single train was run daily from Prescott to Mayer and proved adequate for the shipping volume of the area. However, after the Poland Branch Line was completed, the increased traffic required some changes. A locomotive stationed at Poland made two trips daily from that community and delivered ore destined for the Humboldt smelter to the siding at Poland Junction. At the same time, the P. & E. stationed one locomotive in Mayer and another in Prescott. Each of these trains traveled to the opposite end of the line from where it started and returned to its "home base" daily. The northbound locomotives hauled the ore cars from the siding at Poland Junction to the smelter spur at Humboldt.

Locomotives continued to be stationed at Mayer, Prescott, and Poland after the Crown King Branch reached Middelton. The southbound train from Prescott ran to Middelton before returning to Prescott. This system proved adequate for shipping needs but was a nightmare for the mechanics who maintained the iron horse. Parts were stored and mechanics housed in Mayer, Poland, and the Santa Fe, Prescott and Phoenix yard in Prescott, but this proved expensive and inefficient. After the line was completed to Crown King in 1904, the system was modified once again. All the trains ran out of the S.F., P. & P. yard in Prescott. One train left the yard in Prescott and traveled to Poland before returning home to the engine house at Prescott. A second train left Prescott about an hour after the first and traveled to Crown King, then returned to Prescott. Trains were not always run daily as needs and shipments decreased, but this system was used for several decades on the P. & E. and the B.M. Ry. This method was much more efficient than the earlier experiments, as locomotives were serviced and housed in Prescott where mechanics and parts were readily avaliable. Further, cars from Poland destined for the smelter were only coupled and uncoupled once, and traffic on the lines was controlled much more easily.

The railroad provided a tremendous stimulus to the growth and development of the entire area it served. The impact of the railroad on communities alongside the lines of the P. & E. and the B.M. Ry. can best be studied within the context of the histories of those communities. For more study of those communities, climb aboard as the steam locomotive chugs southward one last time through the rich mining country. Our excursion train will travel the P. & E. and Crown King Line to Crown King. On the return trip to Prescott, which will be late in the day, we'll take time to venture up the track of the Poland Branch. The average speed of the old locomotives on this route was 14 miles per hour, so the excursion will take a full day. We'll meet the engineer at the yard early tomorrow morning and head into mining country and yesteryear.

Preparations begin long before sunrise to ready the old locomotive for the journey. Brass gauges are carefully monitored as the boiler is filled and slowly brought up to operating pressure. It moans and groans with lifelike qualities as it awakens. The engineer methodically oils the driving wheels with his long-snouted oil can and checks for problems. The air is thick with the sounds of powerful machinery and the smells of oil and hot metal. A thin wedge of sun begins to brighten the sky as we board the Bradshaw-bound coach. All aboard! Steam seeps from the cylinders, and with a loud hiss the train lurches forward and slowly begins rolling. The pulsating sound of power and the creaking sound of metal wheels rolling over steel rails pierce the sleepy Prescott morning and enthralls the passengers.

This photograph of the railway yard in Prescott was taken circa 1893. The following photograph was taken about five years later and shows the tremendous growth of operations in Prescott. *Courtesy University of Arizona Special Collections.*

The Santa Fe, Prescott and Phoenix Railway yard in Prescott was the center of operations for the S.F., P. & P. Ry. as well as the P. & E. and B. M. railways. In this photograph, Pea Vine engine No. 9 and P. & E. engines Nos. 10 and 12 rest on the rail near the old engine house. *Courtesy Arizona Department of Library, Archives and Public Records.*

SANTA FE, PRESCOTT & PHŒNIX RAILWAY CO.

TIME TABLE NO. 45.

THROUGH TIME TABLE.

SOUTH BOUND			NORTH BOUND	
2nd class No.3 daily	First class No.1 daily	STATIONS.	First class No.2 daily	2d class No.4 daily
A. M.	P. M.		P. M.	P. M.
5 30	5 35	Lv...Ash Fork...Ar	1 05	6 18
6 00	5 53	.....Meath.....	12 46	5 58
6 23	6 07	....Rock Butte.....	12 33	5 18
6 46				
7 10	6 17	....Cedar Glade.....	12 20	4 47
			P. M.	
7 40	6 34	.....Valley......	12 02	4 14
8 00	6 44	.....Del Rio.....	11 54	4 00
8 25				3 35
9 25	7 00	...Jerome Junction.	11 39	3 07
9 50	7 16	.....Granite......	11 25	2 10
10 15	7 30	..P. & E. Junction..	11 12	2 30
10 40	7 45	.....Prescott.....	10 58	2 10
11 55	7 55		10 48	1 24
P. M.				
12 54	8 25	.....Alto.....	10 25	12 54
12 58	8 29	.....Summit.....	10 22	12 49
1 04	8 35	...Iron Springs...	10 17	12 40
1 12	8 43	..12-Mile Spur..		12 25
			P. M.	
1 28	8 55	.....Ramsgate.....	9 51	12 04
1 53	9 14	...Skull Valley...	9 28	11 33
2 10	9 34	.....Kirkland.....	9 09	11 08
2 35	9 54	...Grand View...	8 51	10 45
3 05	10 09	.....Hillside.....	8 36	10 27
3 22	10 29	...Date Creek...	8 14	10 06
3 47	10 41	.....Piedmont.....	8 02	9 38
4 16				9 15
4 35	11 02	..Congress Junction.	7 46	8 58
5 00				8 30
5 15	11 16	...Harqua Hala...	7 30	8 08
			7 11	7 41
5 46	11 38	....Wickenburg....	6 52	7 14
	A. M.			
6 16	12 06	Hot Springs Junction	6 28	6 43
6 43	12 21	.....Nada.....	6 14	6 25
7 13	12 40	....Beardsley.....	5 56	6 01
7 30	12 57	....Marinette....	5 38	5 42
7 40	1 03	.....Peoria.....	5 32	5 25
7 54	1 12	....Glendale......	5 23	5 12
8 08	1 21	....Alhambra.....	5 14	5 00
P. M.	A. M.		A. M.	A. M.
8 30	1 40	Ar...Phœnix...Lv	5 00	4 40

PRESCOTT & EASTERN.

2d class no 29 daily	2d class no 31 daily	STATIONS.	2d class no 32 daily	2d class no 30 daily
P. M.				
8 30		Lv....Prescott....Ar		7 50
A. M.			P. M.	
9 00		Lv P.&E.Junction Ar		7 35
9 25		.....Yaeger.....		7 20
9 45		...Cherry Creek...		7 05
9 50		...Smelter Spur...		6 44
		....Chaparral....		6 40
10 10		.....Huron.....		6 22
P. M.				
10 15		...Poland Junction.		6 18
10 35				6 00
10 50		Lv....Mayer....Ar		5 48
11 15		.....Cordes.....		5 25
11 50		...Turkey Creek...		4 44
12 10		Ar...Middelton...Lv		4 30
12 35		Ar....Saddle....Lv		4 05
1 35		..Crown King..		2 45p

POLAND BRANCH.

27	—		—	28
A. M.				P. M.
10 10		Lv...Poland J'n...Ar		12 05
10 18		....Henrietta....		11 55
10 25		.....Eugenie.....		11 48
10 35		....Providence....		11 40
10 55		Ar....Poland....Lv		11 25
A. M.				P. M.

This S.F., P. & P. Ry. timetable is dated 12 May 1904 and took effect shortly after the branch line to Crown King was completed.

This timetable is dated 14 October 1903. Note the line was completed to Middelton but did not yet reach Crown King.

Santa Fe, P. & P. R. R. Co.

Time Schedule Now in Force.

SOUTH BOUND			NORTH BOUND	

Prescott & Eastern.

2d class no 25 daily	2d class no 21 daily	STATIONS.	2d class no 24 daily	2d class no 26 daily
P. M.	A. M.		P. M.	P. M.
1 35		Lv...Middelton...Ar		1 20
2 00		...Turkey Creek...		12 55
2 30		.....Cordes.....		12 25
2 55				12 01
3 10	7 00	.....Mayer.....	6 10	11 30
3 30	7 20	..Poland Junction..	5 50	11 10
	9 10		3 45	
3 40	9 15	.....Huron.....	3 40	11 05
		....Chaparral....		
	9 40	...Smelter Spur...	3 22	10 35
4 00	10 15			10 15
4 10	10 20	...Cherry Creek...	3 15	10 05
4 35	10 40	.....Yaeger.....	2 55	9 33
	11 07		2 30	9 00
5 05	11 13	.P. & E. Junction.	2 20	8 50
5 25	11 30	Ar....Prescott....Lv	2 00	8 30

Poland Branch.

A. M.	P. M.		A. M.	P. M.
7 20	3 45	Lv...Poland...Ar	9 10	5 50
7 28	3 54	...Providence...	9 00	5 40
7 35	4 00	.....Eugenie.....		5 33
7 45	4 15	....Henrietta....	8 45	5 25
8 00	4 35	Ar..Poland J'n..Lv	8 30	5 10

H. P. ANEWALT,
General Passenger Agent, Prescott, Ariz.

=The=
Atchison, Topeka & Santa Fe Railway Co.
S. F., P. & P. Lines

TIME TABLE NO. 79

(Superseding Time Table No. 78, in effect Nov. 30, 1919)

To Take Effect Sunday, May 23rd, 1920

AT 12:05 A. M.
Mountain Time

For Information and Government of Employes Only

The Company Reserves the Right to Vary from it at Pleasure
NOTE IMPORTANT CHANGES

This A.T. & S.F. Ry. timetable from May 1920 was the last that specifically listed the S.F., P. & P. lines as a division of the Santa Fe System.

BRANCH LINES

SOUTH BOUND				STATIONS		Side Track Capacity		NORTH BOUND		
Second Class Mixed No. 27 Monday Wednesday and Friday	Second Class Mixed No. 25 Tuesday Thursday and Saturday	Distance From Junction	Fuel and Water		TELEGRAPH CALLS		Telegraph Offices	Second Class Mixed No. 26 Tuesday Thursday and Saturday	Second Class Mixed No. 28 Monday Wednesday and Friday	
8.25 A. M.	8.25 A. M.	.0	Leave	**P. & E. JUNCTION** Arrive		27		6.10 P. M.	3.55 P. M.	
				7.7						
f 8.50	f 8.50	7.7		YAEGER		15		f 5.40	f 3.30	
				7.1						
s 9.10	s 9.10	14.8		CHERRY CREEK	C R	20	D	s 5.15	s 3.05	
				1.8						
s 9.20	s 9.20	16.6	W	HUMBOLDT	B O	106	D	s 5.05	s 2.55	
				3.9						
f 9.40	f 9.40	20.5		HURON Spur		9		f 4.35	f 2.20	
				1.1						
9.45	9.45	21.6		**POLAND JUNCTION**		19		4.30	2.15	
				4.2						
s 10.20	s 10.20	25.8	W	MAYER	MA	42	D	s 4.05	s 1.50	
				2.2						
f 10.30	f 10.30	28.0		BLUE BELL Spur		18		f 3.48	f 1.24	
				2.5						
f 10.50	f 10.50	30.5		CORDES		14		f 3.40	f 1.15	
				7.5						
s 11.20	s 11.20	38.0		TURKEY CREEK Spur		7		s 3.00	s 12.30	
				3.0						
11.45 A. M. Arrive	s 11.45	41.0	W	MIDDELTON		28		s 2.40	12.05 P. M. Leave	
				13.0						
	1.00 P. M.	54.0	W Arrive	**CROWN KING** Leave	C K	30	D	1.20 P. M.		
		.0		**POLAND JUNCTION**		19				
				1.5						
		1.5		HENRIETTA Spur		6				
				1.4						
		2.9		EUGENIE Spur		8				
				1.5						
		4.4	W	PROVIDENCE		9				
				3.5						
		7.9	T	**POLAND**		19				

NOTE—No. 25 has right over No. 26, P. & E. Junction to Crown King.
No. 27 has right over No. 28, P. & E. Junction to Middelton.

LENGTH AND CAPACITY OF TAILS OF SWITCH BACKS
CROWN KING LINE

SWITCH	LENGTH	CAPACITY
1	338.8 ft.	6
2	300.0 "	5
3	336.0 "	6
4	429.3 "	8
5	299.6 "	5
6	429.4 "	8
7	361.0 "	6
8	371.1 "	6
9	422.0 "	8
10	304.0 "	5

These tails hold engine and caboose in addition to cars.

These excerpts are also from A.T. & S.F. timetable No. 79.

We begin our journey on the rail of the Santa Fe, Prescott and Phoenix Railway as we roll out of the depot in Prescott and head north toward the junction of the Prescott and Eastern Line. It takes us about fifteen minutes to steam out of the Prescott yard, past the military post at Fort Whipple, and to the junction with the P. & E. amid the dramatic rock formations of Granite Dells. The switch that directs the rail is unlocked and thrown toward the P. & E., and we prepare to leave the S.F., P. & P. Ry. mainline behind and head into mining country.

Bradshaw Mountain Railway locomotive No. 51 steaming through Granite Dells near Prescott and Eastern Junction. *Courtesy Sharlot Hall Museum.*

The scenery at P. & E. Junction is almost overwhelming in its raw, natural beauty. Carved of granite and sculptured by time, the rocky spires of Granite Dells point toward the heavens. The coarse, brown landscape stands as a tribute to the majesty of "God's Country." Where the rail leaves the S.F.P. & P. and begins its journey toward the Bradshaw Mountains, it passes through a narrow canyon where boulders dominate the rugged terrain and wind whistles among the rocks.

PRESCOTT AND EASTERN JUNCTION
1898 - 1974

Established early in 1898, Prescott and Eastern Junction, as its name implied, was the junction of the steel rail of the P. & E. Ry. with the track of the Santa Fe, Prescott and Phoenix Line. Only a short section of rail was originally laid from the junction and allowed rails, ties, and other construction materials to be delivered for the new railway. A temporary construction camp was built at the junction and served as home for many laborers on the railroad. Supply trains and private coaches of high ranking railway officials rolled through the junction on their way to the end of the shiny rail. As work on the line progressed, the rail was extended and clawed its way to Mayer.

The junction was the center of extensive railroad activity during the initial construction of the P. & E. Ry. and continued as a focal point of considerable rail traffic for several years. The trains of the S.F., P. & P. Ry. ran past the junction as they ventured north from Prescott or south from Ash Fork, and the trains of the P. & E. and B.M. Ry. traveled through the junction on their way to the depot and yard in Prescott. Only six miles from Prescott, the junction was fifty-one miles from Ash Fork and fifty-four miles from the B.M. Ry. terminus in Crown King. Careful scheduling and strict enforcement of operating speeds kept the flow of traffic at P. & E. Junction smooth and orderly.

Several railroad buildings were constructed at P. & E. Junction. A depot was built that faced the Pea Vine and stood just north of the switch that legally started the rail of the P. & E. From that vantage point, traffic on both lines was closely monitored, and train orders were dispatched. A section house and a section workers' bunkhouse were also built at the site. The maintenance crews stationed there had the unenviable task of repairing not only several miles of the S.F., P. & P. track but also maintaining the first eight miles of the P. & E. Line. These crews rode to their daily work on handcars, rain or shine, and regardless of temperature. A siding was constructed a short distance from the depot on the Pea Vine, and another was built behind the depot on the rail of the P. & E. These sidetracks held 21 and 27 cars, respectively, and each was served by small loading platforms.

Traffic on the P. & E. Ry. decreased sharply after the close of World War I, and the lack of activity was evidenced at the P. & E. Junction. Few trains rolled east from the junction as the mining and railroad industries of the Bradshaws were hard hit by the depressed metals market. P. & E. Junction was no longer the center of extensive railroad activity. The depot was removed after the end of World War I, and a short time later the official name of the junction was changed to Entro. The section facilities, although somewhat haggard in appearance, remained in use until 1949 when they were retired.

Today, the rail of the P. & E. has been removed, and the Atchison, Topeka and Santa Fe mainline has been rerouted to a more level right-of-way that bypasses Prescott entirely. The old S.F., P. & P. right-of-way to Prescott receives very little use, and there is talk of abandoning and removing the rail. The roadbed of the P. & E. is still in remarkably good shape and leads from the junction through the granite outcroppings on its way to the historic mining districts. The landscape at the junction remains a scenic wonder and seems to embody the wisdom and beauty of the ages.

This photograph shows the rail of the Santa Fe, Prescott and Phoenix Railway as it approaches P. & E. Junction. The bunkhouse and section house are seen in the distance. The depot and tracks of the P. & E. Ry. are just out of view to the left of the photograph. *Courtesy Arizona Department of Library, Archives and Public Records.*

Left, top: Railroad traffic through Prescott and Eastern Junction was heavy for many years. The engine coming toward us is bound for Ash Fork, while the locomotive behind the depot is headed back to Prescott after a run into the Bradshaw Mountains. *Courtesy Blaine Bowman.* *Left, below:* Granite Dells provides the backdrop in this photograph of Prescott and Eastern Junction. This view is looking south and the rail of the P. &. E. cuts behind the depot to the left. *Courtesy Sharlot Hall Museum.*

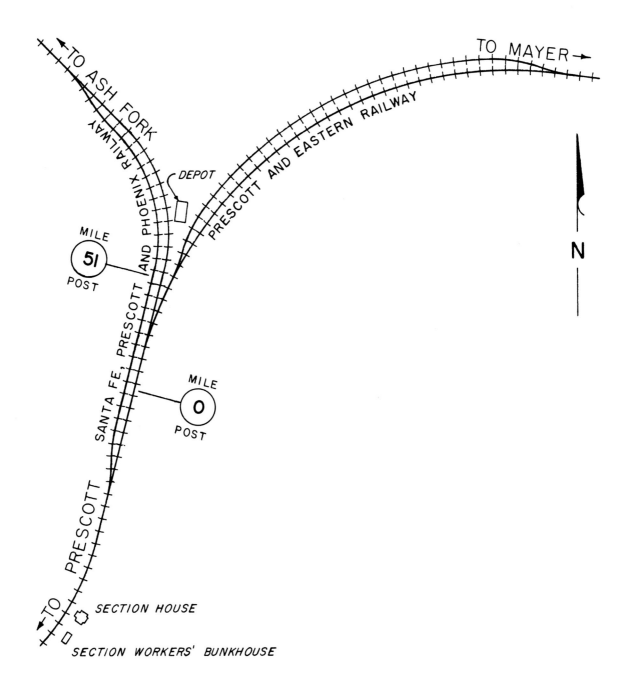

TO ASH FORK ←

TO MAYER →

PRESCOTT AND PHOENIX RAILWAY

PRESCOTT AND EASTERN RAILWAY

DEPOT

MILE **51** POST

SANTA FE, PRESCOTT AND

MILE **0** POST

PRESCOTT

TO ← PRESCOTT

N

SECTION HOUSE

SECTION WORKERS' BUNKHOUSE

PRESCOTT & EASTERN JUNCTION

SCALE: 1" = 250 FEET

MAP BY ROB KROHN

As we travel along the shiny ribbon of steel, an interested passenger can't help but notice the small size of the rail. The distance between the rails is the standard gauge distance of four feet eight and one-half inches, but the rail itself is small and lightweight. The original rail on both the P. & E. and the B.M. Ry. was second-hand, vintage 1880, and was purchased from the Santa Fe Railway. The Santa Fe upgraded and increased the size of its rail throughout the West, and as the old rail was replaced, it was salvaged and sold to other railroads. In the case of the P. & E. and B.M. Ry., the rail was exchanged for stock in those companies. Railroad rail is rated by the weight of a three-foot section of the rail. The rail that was laid during the construction of these branch railroads was lightweight 56-pound rail. The small rail and unusually sharp turns for a standard gauge railroad created a few problems during the railroad's early days of operation as cars frequently "jumped" the tracks. However, as problem areas were identified and safe operating speeds enforced, the derailments were minimized. The size of the rail on the lines was upgraded over the years, first with 65- and later 80- and 90-pound rail. The rail held up well under the strain of the years, and thousands of trains traveled the tracks into mining country.

The rhythmic vibration of our coach over the rail of the P. & E. has brought us to the golden plains of Lonesome Valley to our first stop, Yaeger Siding. In the distance to the northeast, the copper mountains near Jerome rise dramatically into the azure blue sky. A rutted wagon road passes the railroad siding and disappears in the direction of the heralded mining district.

YAEGER SIDING
1898 - 1974

Yaeger Siding was one of the original sidetracks constructed on the Prescott & Eastern Railway and was named for a twisting canyon nearby. Almost eight miles east of P. & E. Junction, the siding was in Lonesome Valley on the old wagon road from Prescott to Jerome. A short distance from the siding, the native grasses of Lonesome Valley led into the brushy brown terrain of Yaeger Canyon.

An ore-loading platform and stockyards stood among the windswept grasses at the siding. Several mines carved copper ore from the walls of Yaeger Canyon, and a few freighted their ore to the siding, but many sent their ore in a different direction to the smelter at Jerome. Although the siding held fifteen cars, ore cars seldom sat on the sidetrack, as ore shipments to Yaeger Siding were neither large nor plentiful.*

The siding was generally a quiet, peaceful place where only the wind tickled the tall grass around the railroad tie fenceposts. The tranquil setting was disturbed for a few days each spring when bellowing cattle were gathered at the stockyards. The cattle pens were the scene of unbridled activity from the fringe of morning light to long after the fireflies flickered in the evening air. The mature cattle, loaded aboard cattle cars, were bound for the dinner tables of a hungry America. The young steers were dehorned, branded with the hot iron, given their shots, and headed for home.

Within a few days, the roundup chores were completed, and the deep-lined faces, dark steel eyes, sweat stained hats, and chew-spattered boots were back on their ranches. Only the wind kicked up corral dust at Yaeger Siding the rest of the year. The sidetrack beneath the massive blue sky served a variety of purposes. On occasion it was even used as a storage yard for damaged or unsafe rolling stock. It remained an interesting location on the railroad for over seventy-five years.

The open fields near the siding were always a highlight for the railroad passengers because of the numerous prairie dog villages there. Hundreds of prairie dogs played like children and scurried about the amber fields. As if on cue, the furry actors stood on their hind legs and looked inquisitively at the trains as they went past. Other wonders of nature were displayed at Yaeger Siding, as the popular prairie dog villages in the foreground were overshadowed by the beauty of endless fields of wild grass against the rugged backdrop of Mingus Mountain.

Yaeger Siding was abandoned by the railroad in March 1974 as the last portion of the old P. & E. was removed from Iron King Spur to Prescott and Eastern Junction. Today, the roadbed of the mainline and Yaeger Siding can still be seen at Yaeger. Little else remains at the site. The prairie dog villages and the old wagon road have all but disappeared into the landscape, and the yearly cattle roundups are nothing more than misty memories.

*Note: The sidetrack capacities on these railways varied slightly over the years; the figures cited in this text are based on timetable No. 79 (23 May 1920). The sidetracks held a locomotive and a caboose in addition to the number of cars stated.

Bradshaw locomotive No. 51 is hard at work on the sidetrack at Yaeger. The small size of the rail is evident in this photograph. *Courtesy Charles Nichols.*

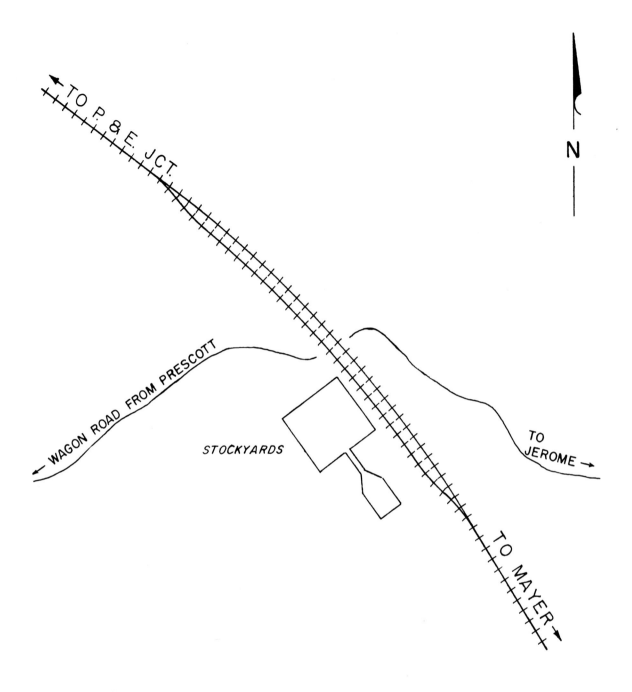

TO P. & E. JCT.

WAGON ROAD FROM PRESCOTT

N

STOCKYARDS

TO JEROME →

TO MAYER →

YAEGER SIDING

SCALE: 1"= 200 FEET

MAP BY ROB KROHN

The second stop on our journey is in the agricultural community of Cherry Creek. The brakes squeal, and the train shudders as we stop alongside the depot. The little railroad depot is the community gathering place where townspeople share news and discuss life. Friendly faces and smiles greet us as we stretch our legs on the depot platform and gaze out upon fields of grain and sweet corn.

CHERRY CREEK STATION

1898 - 1974

The fertile land near the Agua Fria River and Cherry Creek Station attracted settlers long before the Prescott and Eastern Railway was constructed. The first white men in the area found the ruins of ancient Indian dwellings spread out a short distance from the river. The abundance of water and the rich soil soon drew new settlers to the area. Several farms and ranches were established along the river, and a loose-knit community developed. A stage station on the Black Canyon Stage Line and a post office named Agua Frio, later changed to Agua Fria, tied the expansive farms and ranches together, but little else developed.

In 1898, the P. & E. mainline was constructed very close to the Hildebrandt Ranch near the Agua Fria River. A siding was built that served the area and was named Cherry Creek for the large number of wild cherry trees that grew in the vicinity. The siding held twenty cars, was to the west of the mainline, and briefly was the headquarters for the construction crews of the P. & E. Railway. A depot building also built at the siding was one of only three on the original P. & E. Railway. The other two were at Huron and Mayer. The depot building also housed a Wells Fargo office and an office of the Western Union Telegraph Company. It should be noted that both Western Union and Wells Fargo had a blanket contract with the S.F., P. & P. Ry. and its subsidiaries, by which the station agents also represented the telegraph and freight companies.

After the arrival of the railroad, a small hamlet took shape near the siding. A post office was established, but as a post office named Cherry existed only a few miles away, the name Cherry Creek was rejected by the Post Office Department. The name selected by the community for its post office was Dewey. The community was a bit of an oddity in its early days as the post office and the school district were called Dewey, the railroad depot was christened Cherry Creek, and the voting precinct in the town was named Upper Agua Fria. As the years went by, the name most widely recognized for the location was Dewey, but the railroad continued to call the site Cherry Creek.

The community, although not large, had a handful of stores and businesses. In addition to the post office, Wells Fargo, Western Union, and the railway office, a hotel, livery stable, saloon, and a general merchandise store served the little town. Dairy goods, fresh poultry, livestock ranching, and farming were the mainstays of the local economy. The population varied from 100-150 people during most years.

The farmers and ranchers of Cherry Creek had a ready market for their products in nearby Humboldt and elsewhere along the railroad line. Meat, poultry, and tasty vegetables were much sought after in Central Arizona, and the market was large and hungry. The large population of Humboldt bought much of the fresh produce from the fields of

This photograph shows the Cherry Creek Depot, circa 1910. The building in the distance is the Dewey Saloon. *Courtesy Sharlot Hall Museum.*

Cherry Creek as pollutants from the smelter had destroyed the once fertile land at Humboldt.

Although the principal staples of the Cherry Creek economy were farming and ranching, the siding at the community also shipped considerable amounts of gold ore. The hills beyond Cherry Creek were dotted with mining claims and small mines. Several mines produced small to moderate amounts of gold ore, and although total production was not impressive, the railroad shipped the ore and delivered numerous supplies for the mines.

Freight traffic from Cherry Creek Station remained brisk through the 1920s. Passenger traffic, however, was disappointing all along the Prescott and Eastern Line. The depot building at Cherry Creek was quiet and was badly needed elsewhere on the Santa Fe System. The railway company moved the building from Cherry Creek to Skull Valley west of Prescott on 6 April 1926. The siding at Cherry Creek, although seldom used after the thirties, remained along the mainline until 1974. In that year, the mainline and all sidings and spurs along the old P. & E. were abandoned and removed by the Santa Fe Railway.

Today, Cherry Creek or Dewey remains a peaceful little farming and ranching community. Weeds and grass grow on the once solid roadbed, but the old mainline and siding are still clearly visible along state highway 69 at Dewey. Sweet corn, squash, and melons abound in the dark, rich soil. The Cherry Creek depot still stands at Skull Valley, where it has been moved to private land and is being restored by the historical society of that community.

The Cherry Creek Depot sat along the tracks at Skull Valley for many years. This photograph was taken more than three decades after the small building was moved to its new location in 1926. *Courtesy Charles Wolz.*

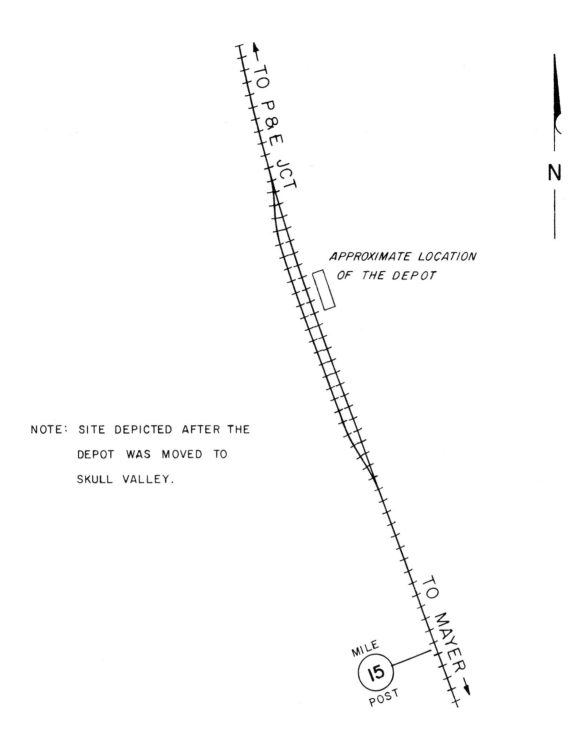

TO P&E JCT

N

APPROXIMATE LOCATION
OF THE DEPOT

NOTE: SITE DEPICTED AFTER THE
DEPOT WAS MOVED TO
SKULL VALLEY.

TO MAYER

MILE
15
POST

CHERRY CREEK STATION

SCALE: 1"= 250 FEET

MAP BY ROB KROHN

It's a short distance to our next stop, Humboldt. The engineer slows the locomotive, and we roll to a stop alongside the tidy, little Humboldt depot. A long, green baggage cart sits empty on the depot platform, and we exchange pleasantries with the personable station agent. The local postmaster takes delivery of a bag of mail and delights the crew with an account of his recent fishing trip. To the east of the depot, the smelter smokestack reaches high into the air and belches thick smoke.

HUMBOLDT STATION
1905 - 1974

The land where Humboldt was founded in 1906 already had a rich history long before the twentieth century. Adjacent to the Agua Fria River at Humboldt and farther north near Cherry Creek, Indians dwelled upon and cultivated the land 700 years before the steel-plated thunder served the area. The first white settlers to the area in the 1860s found ruins of ancient rock houses and ceremonial pits crumbling along the river. At a time when attacks from live Indians were not uncommon, the settlers used the remnants of the rock walls in the construction of solid, new houses and livestock shelters. Self-preservation, not historic preservation, was the code of the day.

As it churned and cut within its banks behind Humboldt, the Agua Fria River was ideal for powering an ore mill. Levi Bashford, who later became a prominent Prescott merchant, was aware of the area's potential and established a mill site at the location in the late 1860s. The mill site, known as the Bashford or Agua Fria Mill, processed ore from early discoveries in the Bradshaw foothills. The mill was not a large one, and only small to moderate amounts of ore were processed.

When the Prescott and Eastern Railway was constructed to Mayer, it passed one and one-half miles west of the mill site. There was little activity at the location in 1898, but that was about to change. The Valverde Smelting Company acquired the mill site and a large tract of adjacent property in

1899. This company constructed a large smelter, laid out and built a town for its employees, and convinced the P. & E. Railway that a spur was needed at the new facility. In the heat of early July 1899, surveyors for the P. & E. Ry. were in the field and located the best route for the roadbed. Construction on the one and one-half mile spur started immediately and was pushed rapidly. On 5 August the crews started laying rail and completed their work on what was called the Smelter Spur late the same month. The railroad crews were not the only construction workers hard at work at the site.

The town that was planned near the smelter grew up almost overnight. Ground was broken for the smelter and town in July 1899, and by year's end not only was the smelter in operation, but several other structures were completed at the site. Many more buildings were under construction as the winds of fall teased the brightly colored surveyor's ribbons and stakes that marked the landscape. The sound of carpenters' hammers were heard throughout the winter and spring months as houses and shops went up. The town was named Valverde for the company that owned the site. A post office was established in the new community on 24 November 1899, and the possibilities seemed unlimited.

The Valverde smelter, along with the railroad, was what mining in the Bradshaw Mountains desperately needed. No longer were ore shipments

The Valverde smelter was a long-awaited and welcome addition to the Bradshaw Mountain mining industry. This photograph, taken at the turn of the century, shows the furnace in full operation. *Courtesy Arizona Historical Foundation, Hayden Library, Arizona State University.*

This view of the Humboldt smelter shows the plant circa 1910. *Courtesy Camp Verde Historical Society.*

sent as far away as El Paso, San Francisco, and Colorado to be processed. Carloads of ore arrived at the local smelter as soon as it was completed. As investment capital poured into the mining region, shiny metal was poured from the furnace. The branch lines of the Bradshaw Mountain Railway to Poland and Crown King brought in more ore than the smelter was able to handle. The daily capacity was 250 tons, and plans were unveiled in early 1904 to double the size of the plant.

The expansion plans met a fiery end on 28 September 1904, when flames engulfed the smelter and nearby buildings. Flames leaped high into the sky, and onlookers stared in helpless disbelief as the fire consumed the smelter that held so much promise. Charred timbers and soot-covered corrugated roofing smoldered in a disheartening heap. Only $60,000 insurance was carried on the $160,000 facility, and funds were not available to rebuild. The fortunes of fate turned quickly, and for the second time in the area's history, the local inhabitants moved elsewhere.

The site was dormant for almost a year while financiers and investors created a new company and formalized construction plans for a new smelter at the location. This plant was funded by the Arizona Smelting Company, which was owned in large part by Frank Murphy, his associates, and the Santa Fe Railway. Construction began in September 1905 on the new smelter, which was much larger and more efficiently planned than the original structure. Work progressed rapidly on the new facility as masons, carpenters, and other skilled tradesmen displayed their talents at the site. Within a month, buildings had risen like magic from the ashes of Valverde. Not only was the smelter itself much larger than its predecessor, the new townsite and railroad facilities that served the area were also greatly expanded.

The newest townsite was laid out along the railroad tracks a little farther west than the Valverde townsite. The proximity of the business and residential districts to the railroad tracks was convenient and provided a one-half mile buffer zone from the smoke and noise of the smelter. The P. & E. Ry. constructed a wye at the site, which conveniently allowed the trains to change direction with little difficulty and also permitted easy access to the smelter by north and southbound trains. The wye served as the focal point of the business part of town, as a railroad depot was built within the wye and store buildings lined its stems. The depot building was completed late in 1905, and within a few weeks it was flanked by stores, restaurants, barber shops, and lodging houses.

Railroad construction crews worked on assorted building projects at the site well into 1906. More than 125 men labored on several miles of new railroad track. The rail, directed by twenty-nine switches, twisted through the townsite and among the various smelter buildings. The network of sidetracks in the community held a total of 106 cars and crisscrossed the landscape. After the railroad carpenters completed the depot building, they started on a bunkhouse for the railroad's maintenance crew, a section house, tool house, water tank, loading platforms, ore bins, and three buildings that were leased to local merchants.

On 18 August 1905, the new community was christened Humboldt. Some writers have stated that the community was named for Baron Alexander Von Humboldt, who visited Northern Mexico in the 18th century. An equally strong, but less romantic, case can be presented that some of the founders of the community had roots in Humboldt, California, and thus proposed the name. Whatever the origin of its name, the community

Passengers await the northbound train at the Humboldt Depot in the summer of 1914. Notice the north portion of the wye and one of the town's many railroad switches in the distance. *Courtesy Mynne Jarman.*

This store was near the depot in Humboldt. It was owned by the railroad and leased for several years to merchant Charles P. Wingfield. *Courtesy Margaret Hallett.*

rapidly grew and surpassed Mayer, Poland, and Crown King as the center of mining and railroading in the mountains south of Prescott. The local post office and merchants were soon supported by more than 1,000 residents, and the town swelled with new arrivals almost daily.

In 1906, as workers and their families settled in Humboldt, merchants rushed to the burgeoning town. Wells Fargo and Western Union were among the first businesses established at Humboldt and were located in the railroad depot. Within the next year, ten saloons, five restaurants, five general stores, three hotels, and three mining companies had opened their doors in the community. Several other businessmen soon arrived and offered their goods and services in the bakeries, meat markets, drug stores, photographic studios, billiard halls, livery stables, barber shops, and jewelry store in Humboldt. The townspeople were proud of their hospital, doctor's office, justice of the peace, and Congregational Church, each of which added a sense of permanence and respectability to their community.

Several other urban refinements were present in Humboldt. The local school district was created in 1906 with forty-three children and a one-room schoolhouse. The number of school children in the district more than doubled in the next two years, and in 1908 the residents of Humboldt helped raise $3,500 for the construction of a large brick schoolhouse. The two schoolhouses contained slightly more than one-hundred desks and students in 1908 and continued to grow. The new schoolhouse was also used as the polling place for the Humboldt Voting Precinct. The voting booths at the school were crowded, as voting was popular during general elections. The registered voters studied the issues and candidates just as rigorously as the school children studied their lessons. The new schoolhouse was also among the first Humboldt buildings served by a local water company. Many of the buildings relied on shallow wells as their source of water. Other public utilities enjoyed in the town were electricity and telephone service.

The town was very pleased with its rapid progress, and to showcase its development it hosted the local Labor Day celebration for 1907. More than 1,000 people traveled to Humboldt and participated in the festivities. The railroad added cars to the regular trains and also ran special

41

This is downtown Humboldt, Arizona. The building at the far right is the post office. *Courtesy Arizona Department of Library, Archives and Public Records.*

excursion trains that brought celebrants to the community. The traditional parade, complete with marching band, started the day of celebration, and there was something for everyone. The children enjoyed footraces, burro races, and pie eating contests. The adults watched and joined in horse races, baseball games, rock drilling contests, bronco busting, and the ever popular food tasting events. A grand ball in the old schoolhouse capped off the long day, and weary, but happy, travelers boarded the railroad coaches and headed home in the early hours of the morning.

Humboldt continued to grow and prosper as long as the smelter was in operation. The De Soto and Blue Bell Mines were owned by the same company as the smelter and were the largest contributors of ore to the plant, but ore was processed from innumerable mines throughout Arizona. Humboldt and its smelter were at the mercy of mine production and the national metals market. The smelter was closed on several occasions owing to a shortage of ore that was the result of low market

value of the metals. Late in 1907 and again in 1911, the smelter closed for extended periods of time. Dozens of empty railroad cars sat on the tracks near the silent smelter, and residents only hoped conditions would improve before they had to go elsewhere in search of work. The periods of shutdown were frustrating, but the town rebounded from the adversity and again prospered during World War I.

Amazing quantities of ore were processed at Humboldt during the war years. Locomotives pulled long trains of ore cars into the smelter town and then carried loads of metal back to Prescott and to manufacturing centers throughout the country. There was so much railroad activity at Humboldt that two switch locomotives were stationed in the yard to move cars from sidetrack to sidetrack. The large locomotives traveled the mainline and delivered the cars to the sidetracks; the smaller engines then jockeyed the cars to their specific destinations at the smelter facility. The switch locomotives also gathered the cars that were headed back toward the mineral-rich slopes and placed them where the more powerful engines simply coupled to the line of cars and headed south. Adroit administration of the railroad yard and the smelter and the great demand for copper enabled nearly 1,000 tons of ore to be processed each day at Humboldt. In July 1916, the railroad yard handled 374 cars of freight. Twelve months later that figure had risen to 559 cars. As the hundreds of ore cars rolled into town, more than 2,000,000 pounds of pure copper left the smelter each month.

After the war ended, metal prices dropped, and ore shipments decreased sharply. The effect on the town was minimal at first, but over the next several years the community suffered greatly. In 1920, the population was 900 people, diminished about 25 percent from the bustling days of World War I. The saloons were shut down by prohibition, and the business sector struggled to stay in the black. The Humboldt movie theatre continued to draw a good crowd as the popularity of motion pictures increased, but other local businesses did not experience the same success. The Humboldt Branch of the Prescott State Bank felt the economic shortfall in its cash drawers and reluctantly closed its vault for the last time. The smelter remained closed for most of the decade, and hopes of a return to prosperity faded among the townspeople. Many workers, merchants, and even the Congregational Church lost faith in the community and left during the twenties. The population dwindled to less than 500 by 1930, and the outlook was not optimistic. Rusted rails that longed for traffic and bleached, gray storefronts that cried for business marked the twenties and thirties.

Although the nearby Iron King Mine was reopened in the thirties. Humboldt did not experience the resurgence that many expected. The mine produced large amounts of ore, and some of the workers lived in Humboldt, but a much smaller work force lived in the town than during the hectic days of World War I. Many of the employees at the mine lived in Prescott and commuted sixteen miles to work rather than live in Humboldt. Very little of the ore mined at the Iron King was processed at Humboldt, as the old smelter was not equipped for

the mine's complex ore. Some of the old smelter facility had been removed as early as 1927, and most of what remained was dismantled ten years later. The mines that remained in operation, including the Iron King, sent their ore on the railroad to the United Verde smelter of Phelps Dodge at Clarkdale, to the Magma Copper Company smelter at Superior, or to the American Smelting and Refining Company smelter at Hayden.

The exodus that began slowly with the close of World War I continued through the forties and fifties. In 1941, only four hundred people called Humboldt their home. Advances in mining technology and heavy machinery made it possible to increase production with less manpower. The railroad shipped large quantities of ore from the Iron King to smelters throughout Arizona, but little traffic was recorded in Humboldt. Much of the labyrinth of railroad track at Humboldt was abandoned and removed in the thirties and forties.

When the Iron King Mine was exhausted in 1968, little of the old town of Humboldt remained. Most of the original mining and railroad buildings had burned or had been razed for safety and tax purposes years before. The last of the original smelter smokestacks became a hazard and, as a small gathering of old-timers watched, was dynamited to the ground in 1955. The old stack was one of the tallest in the Southwest and in many ways symbolized the end of an era at Humboldt. Like the smelter itself, the railroad depot, the falsefront stores, and the white-haired men that ran them, the smokestack faded into memory.

Today, only a couple of old falsefront buildings and a barren cemetery overlooking town remain at Humboldt. A smelter smokestack still stands which, although confused by many as an old stack, was actually constructed well into the twentieth century. Most of the railroad grade through town is still plainly visible and covered with black cinders. The site of the railroad depot is easily located and overlooks the playground of the new school. Small ranches and mobile homes are scattered between the abandoned roadbed of the old P. & E. and the banks of the dry Agua Fria River.

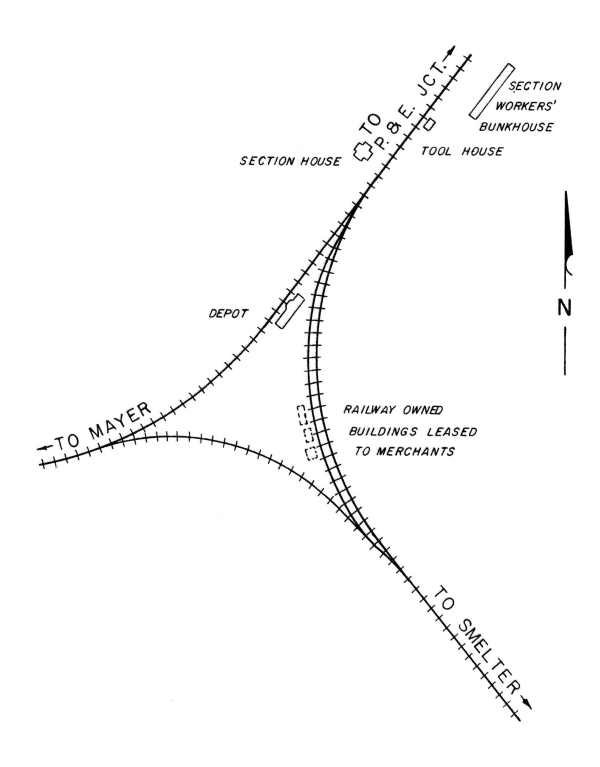

SECTION WORKERS' BUNKHOUSE

TO P. & E. JCT.

TOOL HOUSE

SECTION HOUSE

N

DEPOT

TO MAYER

RAILWAY OWNED
BUILDINGS LEASED
TO MERCHANTS

TO SMELTER

HUMBOLDT STATION

SCALE: 1"= 200 FEET

MAP BY ROB KROHN

Just over a half-mile south of the Humboldt depot is the Iron King Spur. Gallows headframes and mine buildings spread across the open foothills to the west of the tracks. Smoke billows from the hoisting plant, and the pounding of mining equipment resounds through the landscape. Ore samples lay in piles beside the assay office and await testing as our locomotive steams past the short railroad spur that serves the mine.

IRON KING SPUR

1903 - 1974

The Iron King Spur was named for and served the mine of that name. The mine was a discovery that dated to the 1880s, but little work was done there prior to the turn of the century. Early mining activity at the property concerned iron, as the mine's name indicates, along with copper, gold, and silver. Some small to moderate early production was recorded at the mine, but investors were not interested in a "marginal" property when there were more promising investments. The owners of the mine did as much selling of stock and promotion of the property as they did actual mining. The promoters convinced the Prescott and Eastern Railway that both companies needed a railroad spur at the mine. In 1903, the P. & E., completed a short spur that served the mining property.

The Iron King Spur was only a flagstop for its first three decades on the line. The train stopped only if a "flag" was raised at the spur which signalled that a car full of ore was ready to be shipped. The spur was to the west of the mainline, had its connection on the north end of the spur, and held four cars. Although the Iron King Mine remained open and active throughout World War I, shipments of ore from the mine were small and inconsistent. When the Iron King Mine and Humboldt smelter closed after the war, the spur was quickly forgotten and overgrown. It was abandoned but not removed by the railroad in the summer of 1922. The spur was re-established in November 1926 after the mine reopened, but the shipments were once again small.

A small camp developed at the Iron King Mine at the turn of the century. The camp was originally called Blanchard and honored the mine superintendent at the property. A post office, also named Blanchard, was established at the mine in August 1903. The name of the post office was changed to Iron King in 1907, but within five years the office had been closed. By 1912, Humboldt had grown to the extent that little more than the railroad tracks and the Phoenix to Prescott road separated the Iron King Mine from the town. Most of the miners at the mine lived in Humboldt, and the stores and post office in that community were utilized.

A new era in the history of the Iron King Mine began in 1934. Technological advances in the mining industry, an upswing in the metals market, and keen management resulted in unprecedented prosperity at the Iron King. The importance of lead and zinc as industrial metals increased throughout the thirties and rose dramatically during World War II when the commodities were used for military purposes. Production at the mine reached amazing levels after the deposits of lead and zinc at the mine were realized to be virtually limitless. The mine produced almost five hundred tons of ore per day during World War II, and this figure increased to over one thousand tons per day in the 1950s.

The Iron King Spur was enlarged to handle the increased volume of the ore shipments and no longer was a flagstop. The spur was far and away the busiest on the old P. & E. line after the mid-thirties, when the Iron King became the largest zinc and lead mine in Arizona. The mine was finally exhausted in 1968 but produced more than $160,000,000 worth of ore, all but $100,000 of that after 1936. The railroad spur remained alongside the deserted mine until 1962, when it was removed. The mainline remained at the location into 1974, when it retreated back to Prescott and Eastern Junction.

Today, the roadbed of both the railroad mainline and Iron King Spur can still be seen southwest of Humboldt. Several vacant buildings huddle at the Iron King Mine, badly in need of paint and repair. The assayer of the Iron King still hangs his shingle on the assay office and is open to the general public for business. The barren wasteland of the dried tailings pond and yellowish soil dominate the depressing landscape at the Iron King.

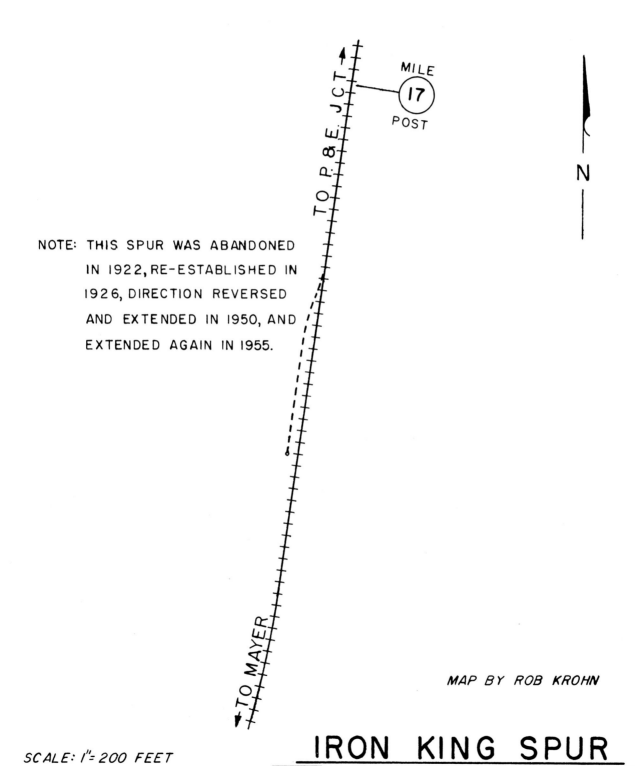

MILE
17
POST

TO P.&E. JCT.

N

NOTE: THIS SPUR WAS ABANDONED IN 1922, RE-ESTABLISHED IN 1926, DIRECTION REVERSED AND EXTENDED IN 1950, AND EXTENDED AGAIN IN 1955.

TO MAYER

MAP BY ROB KROHN

SCALE: 1"= 200 FEET

IRON KING SPUR

Just over three miles beyond Humboldt we approach Chaparral Spur. Several ore cars, two cars full of coal, and a boxcar sit on the rail. As we reach the sidetrack, we can see dry goods destined for the Flammer General Store at McCabe being carried from the boxcar to a wagon by two men and a young boy. The hillsides beyond are covered with dense chaparral, and the brush thicket grows within a few feet of the railroad spur.

CHAPARRAL SPUR

1898 - 1922

Chaparral Spur was constructed in 1898 and was one of the original locations on the Prescott and Eastern Line. Located near the gulch of the same name, Chaparral Spur was constructed one-half mile north of the depot and crowded siding at Huron. The spur, elevation 4,779 feet, was very active during the early days after the P. & E. was completed to Mayer. It was to the west of the mainline, was 669 feet long, and had its connection with the mainline on the north end of the sidetrack. A 375 foot long, three level, ore chute was built alongside the spur and simplified the task of loading ore into the railroad's ore cars. The lower portion of the platform was used when freight was unloaded at the spur.

Chaparral Spur served nearby mines and the towns of Chaparal and McCabe. The town of Chaparal, which was spelled differently than the railroad spur, was four miles west of the spur in the rugged country near the Little Jessie Mine. The town grew in size in the 1890s after several other mineral discoveries were made nearby. The town had the usual assortment of livery stable, hotel, saloon, and general merchandise store and opened a post office in 1894. The town rapidly grew to two hundred people as local mines produced considerable quantities of gold and silver ore. A good road led from the town to Chaparral Spur, and the mine operators and merchants made extensive use of the railroad sidetrack.

The town of McCabe was two miles west of both Chaparral Spur and Huron Siding. Most ore shipments from mines near that community went to Huron, although some of the smaller mines freighted ore to Chaparral Spur. Some McCabe merchants received shipments at Chaparral Spur, as the siding at Huron was often too crowded for boxcars of merchandise to sit there for several days until unloaded. The proprietor of the largest general merchandise store in McCabe, George Flammer, made extensive use of Chaparral Spur and stocked his shelves with supplies received there.

On 31 March 1905, a tragic accident occurred at Chaparral Spur. Poor communication between the engineer and brakeman may have caused the calamity. As cars on the spur were being coupled and uncoupled, the brakeman was crushed between two cars. The injured man was rushed to a Prescott hospital, but there was little that could be done. The railroad community joined the brakeman's family and mourned the loss of a good friend and a fine man.

On the fateful March day when the accident occurred, ten cars stood on Chaparral Spur. Coal cars, five in number and with cargo headed for mines near Chaparal, dominated the spur. A flat car loaded with mining equipment and a boxcar full of heavy machinery earmarked for mines near Chaparal also sat on the spur. Destined for McCabe were boxcars of goods owned by merchant George Flammer and a boxcar of mining supplies consigned by Brown Brothers Hardware of Prescott.

The mines near Chaparal and McCabe waned about 1907, and most were totally exhausted by

This photograph of McCabe shows the community spread through Galena Gulch. Chaparral Spur was nearly two miles in the distance, while Huron and its railroad siding were beyond the hill to the right. *Courtesy Sharlot Hall Museum.*

1912. The mines served by Chaparral Spur were primarily gold and silver producers and did not experience the tremendous stimulation from World War I that the producers of strategic metals like copper received. Although a few mines struggled and clung to life, the area around both Chaparal and McCabe was almost deserted. The neglected look and ghost-like appearance of Chaparal and McCabe were also in evidence at Chaparral Spur, where only tumbleweeds and an occasional coyote crossed the rail. The mines near Chaparral Spur were either closed, exhausted, or both by 1920, and the spur had a forlorn and pitiful appearance by that time.

The days of Chaparral Spur were numbered. The ore-loading chute was torn down, and the spur was shortened to two-car capacity. In 1922, Santa Fe Railway officials decided that Chaparral Spur was no longer needed and removed it in June of that year.

Today, the mainline near Chaparral Spur can still be seen. The roadbed of the spur, however, has been destroyed by the hands of time and the machinery of progress. Recent grading of a road from the location has destroyed the last traces of the spur that for nearly a quarter-of-a-century was one of the busiest on the old Prescott and Eastern Railway.

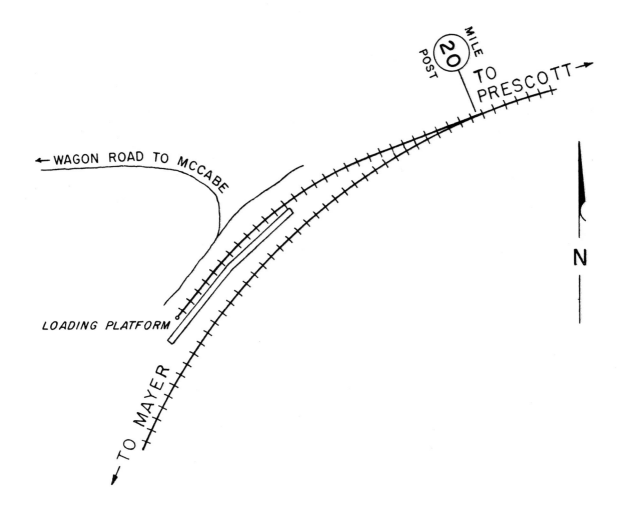

CHAPARRAL SPUR

SCALE: 1" = 200 FEET   MAP BY ROB KROHN

The next stop on our southbound excursion over the P. & E. Ry. is at Huron. As we near the community, we see great activity on the town's short railroad siding. Teamsters are loading mining equipment aboard freight wagons bound for McCabe. Other teamsters are unloading ore wagons of mineral destined for the smelter.

HURON STATION

1898 - 1928

The route of the Prescott and Eastern Railway was carefully orchestrated by Frank Murphy and his associates to cross several mining properties in which they held large financial interests. Survey crews began locating right-of-way for the P. & E. in late 1897 and, by the next fall, the rail was nearing Joe Mayer's stage station on the Black Canyon Route. The rail crossed near one of Murphy's mining properties, the Huron Mine.

This group of mining claims was a surprisingly late discovery considering its proximity to the stage route from Phoenix to Prescott. The area had been well-prospected, as it lay less than two miles east of the famous McCabe Mine and within walking distance of many smaller mines. The Huron claims, the first of which was filed in 1896, appeared to be surface outcroppings which would inevitably diminish below ground. However, that theory was soon dispelled by a mining misfortune at the property. Working near the bottom of a shallow shaft, the miners hit water, and the shaft began to flood. Fearing for their safety, the men left their tools and climbed out of the shaft. Upon their return several days later, they found the mineral-rich water had turned their tools into almost pure copper. Assay figures on the first samples taken from this shaft were as high as 65 percent copper with some spectacular gold specimens. Word of the discovery spread, and several nearby claims were either filed or purchased.

Murphy quickly secured a bond on the Huron property, erected a camp, and began operating twenty-four hour shifts to develop the mine. Among others owning claims near Murphy was William Hull. Hull, it should be noted, was one of the developers of the United Verde and United Verde Extension Mines at Jerome, Arizona. Although the Huron discoveries did not prove to be part of a rich mineral belt like the discoveries in Jerome, the properties yielded gold and copper ores of moderate mineral wealth. The outlook for the Huron Group of mines was still optimistic in 1898 as the railroad construction crews laid rail across claims on the recently acquired right-of-way.

The town of Huron was created by the railroad. It built a small depot, warehouse, and siding near the Huron group and named the depot and siding in their honor. The laborers employed in the construction of the twenty-six-mile Prescott and Eastern Line were primarily single men coarse of character and dry of throat. Recognizing the needs of these men and the opportunity before him, Charles P. Wingfield, an enterprising young man who had been employed by the P. & E. Ry., established a saloon near the depot at Huron. The saloon opened in October 1898 and proved so popular that Wingfield soon planned to stock a general merchandise store.

Wingfield was no stranger to the general merchandise business, as his family had been involved in the mercantile and cattle businesses in the Verde Valley for many years. Robert W. Wingfield assisted his brother in his fledgling businesses, and together they built an extensive mercantile concern. They not only operated the

Charles P. Wingfield, the first merchant to hang his shingle in Huron. *Courtesy Margaret Hallett.*

The road from Huron, in the center foreground, led into the business district of nearby McCabe. *Courtesy Sharlot Hall Museum.*

The Cabinet Saloon, although in nearby McCabe and not in Huron, was representative of the time period. *Courtesy Arizona Historical Foundation, Hayden Library, Arizona State University.*

saloon but also supplied lumber, livestock, feed, mining supplies, general merchandise, firewood, and housing and owned the local hotel. In addition, they employed teamsters to transport supplies from the railroad siding to outlying mining camps.

By the turn of the century, it was apparent that Huron's economic future lay not in the direct discovery of rich ore at its mines but in supplying materials to other mining camps—most notably McCabe. McCabe was a large camp two miles northwest of Huron that supported four to six hundred people during its peak years, 1900 to 1907. This camp was without the luxury of rail service and relied heavily upon Huron's nine-car capacity railroad siding to receive supplies and ship ore to the smelter.

While the mines of McCabe boomed, so did the businesses of Huron. After the railroad line was completed to Mayer, C.P. Wingfield sold his saloon to Frank Nester and concentrated his efforts in the lumber, mercantile, and meat market businesses. Wingfield soon ran forty head of cattle on his land at Huron and owned and operated a fresh meat market at McCabe. The saloon continued to be a small but profitable concern, and Nester poured many a drink.

The dark, hardwood bar in the Huron saloon, worn smooth by the leaning of elbows, heard many tales of misfortune over the years. One of the old tales that has endured, for whatever reasons, follows. Railroad handcars, pulled by horses or burros, were often used by small groups to travel to other towns along the tracks. It seems a family was returning home late one night from a dance in a nearby community. As the handcar was pulled over a particularly desolate section of rail, one of the ladies thought she heard a moan. The group continued down the rail, and soon a painful cry pierced the crisp night air. With hand lanterns, the men searched the darkness for the source of the chilling scream. A short distance from the tracks they discovered a grizzly sight. They found a blood-drenched and dirt covered man with his brains literally beat out.

Apparently the man, a miner, had been paid two weeks' wages and was heading toward town. He was approached by two men who asked if they could walk into town with him. After traveling for some distance, one of the men picked up a rock and hit the miner in the back of the head. He was brutally beaten, robbed, kicked into a shallow grave, and left for dead. Delirious, he managed to drag himself from the grave and crawl several feet to where he was found. He was loaded onto the handcar and taken into town. A train was dispatched to carry the injured man to the hospital in Prescott. Throughout the night, the man screamed, "I'll get the two who done it." During the weeks of treatment in the hospital and sanitarium, those were the only words he mumbled. He never recovered from his injuries and died a few months later.

This family is on a railroad handcar traveling to a nearby town. Judging by their appearance, they were headed to a social function. *Courtesy Charles Nichols.*

Legend had it that, late at night, the miner's spirit filled the countryside with bloodcurdling cries and searched for "the two who done it." Saloon patrons in Huron, as well as other Bradshaw Mountain towns, debated whether the ghost of the victim haunted the areas nearby.

In addition to the saloon and the concerns of Wingfield, other businesses were represented in Huron. The P. & E. Ry. was not the only large company with an office in the community. When the railway began operations in Huron, the Western Union Telegraph Company and Wells Fargo opened offices in the depot. The small railroad depot, which only measured sixty-four by twenty feet, was not cramped for space as the same agent served all three companies.

Essential public utilities and services were available in Huron. A small post office, established in 1901, served the community for more than a quarter-of-a-century. Telephone service was provided by the Prescott Electric Company and connected Huron with most camps in the area as well as the social and cultural center of Prescott. Electric power was available from the same company, but like telephone service was utilized primarily by large companies and not the general population. The county created the Huron School District in 1902. The district remained active into 1904 when, due to small enrollment, it was absorbed into the McCabe School District.

The Yavapai County Sheriff did not assign a deputy to the little community; however, his men in nearby McCabe, Mayer, Humboldt, and Poland could be called upon when law enforcement was necessary. Although most of the citizenry was law-abiding and the sheriff was not needed very often, his services were called upon by an angry Charles Wingfield in early 1902. The following excerpt from the *Prescott Weekly Courier* addresses the Wingfield complaint.

> Mr. and Mrs. Hornbuckle, of McCabe, went to Phoenix a few days ago. Charley Wingfield of the McCabe meat market firm of Wingfield & Hornbuckle has sworn out a warrant charging Hornbuckle with getting away with from $400 to $500 of the firm's money. Hornbuckle has been arrested in Phoenix and will be brought to Prescott today. He will be accompanied by his wife.

This was a relatively rare situation, as most disagreements were amicably resolved locally. The majority of the sheriff's visits were social ones.

Recreation in Huron was similar to that in other local camps. Hunting was popular, as were card playing, reading, dancing, and storytelling. Old-fashioned "fiddlin" music and pot-luck dinners were the biggest attractions. The McCabe Miner's Union and other fraternal organizations in that community were very active in promoting dances and social events. After McCabe began to decline,

These young men and women "walked the rail" on their way to Humboldt in the summer of 1914. *Courtesy Mynne Jarman.*

Humboldt and Mayer hosted the dances, dinners, and miscellaneous celebrations. All these communities were within short distances of Huron and provided the organized social and recreational activities so enjoyed by the residents of the community.

Shallow wells and natural springs provided all the water needed by the town. Springs dotted the Huron area, and thus obtaining water was not a problem. On one occasion, a spring suddenly appeared in the middle of the road from Huron to McCabe and necessitated permanent rerouting around the muddy area.

The population of Huron was always small, as the town was primarily a supply center for the surrounding mines and camps. The voter registration rolls show twelve listings for the camp in early 1904. The November election results show fifteen voters in 1904 and twenty-two in 1906. The local schoolmarm taught ten students during the 1902-1903 school year. These figures were the highest ever enjoyed by the one-room schoolhouse. By 1908, the Huron population dwindled to sixteen.

Although several mines were later located in the immediate area of Huron, none of any consequence developed. The economy of Huron was totally dependent upon supplying mining operations to the west; the fortunes of the small settlement slowly faded as operations there did. After McCabe's mines closed, Huron's fate was decided, and it fulfilled its destiny.

The first year of Arizona statehood found Huron badly neglected. An occasional hopper-bottom ore car still stood on the siding, but the depot was no longer used, and the original merchants had all sold out. Some of the Huron residents, like Charles Wingfield, established residences and businesses up the tracks in neighboring Humboldt, while others moved to the growing metropolitan areas of Prescott and Phoenix. The Huron Voting Precinct was discontinued in 1912. The few people who remained had to go to Humboldt to vote. The post office remained open to serve miners and others who optimistically believed that another rich lode would be discovered near McCabe. Other merchants replaced those who left, but Huron's days were unmistakably numbered.

Huron did enjoy a brief resurgence during World War I when the Big Ledge Copper Company and the Big Ledge Extension Mining Company reopened mines near town. The mines in the hills to the west made the small railroad siding the scene of activity once again. Nearly one hundred people received their mail at the Huron Post Office in 1919. This figure is misleading, as few of those were Huron residents. Most were from camps west of Huron, including McCabe, where the post office had been discontinued. The signing of the Armistice that ended World War I brought to a close the lucrative price supports and great demand for ore production which had revived mining in the Big Bug area. Hopes of renewed prosperity returned to Huron, only to leave almost as rapidly as they came. The post office managed to keep its doors open until 30 November 1928, when it was discontinued. Local residents then received their mail in Mayer.

Weeds, rotted wood, and rusted rail soon marked the site of the little town. In the late twenties, the railroad dismantled its depot and warehouse for tax purposes. It removed its rail and legally abandoned its line through Huron in 1958. The eroded railroad grade that slowly winds its way uphill toward the silent smelter town of Humboldt and downhill toward the small settlement started by Joe Mayer holds the heart of a bygone day. The town of Huron, save the old depot grade and brush-covered barrel hoops, has been claimed by the Big Bug countryside.

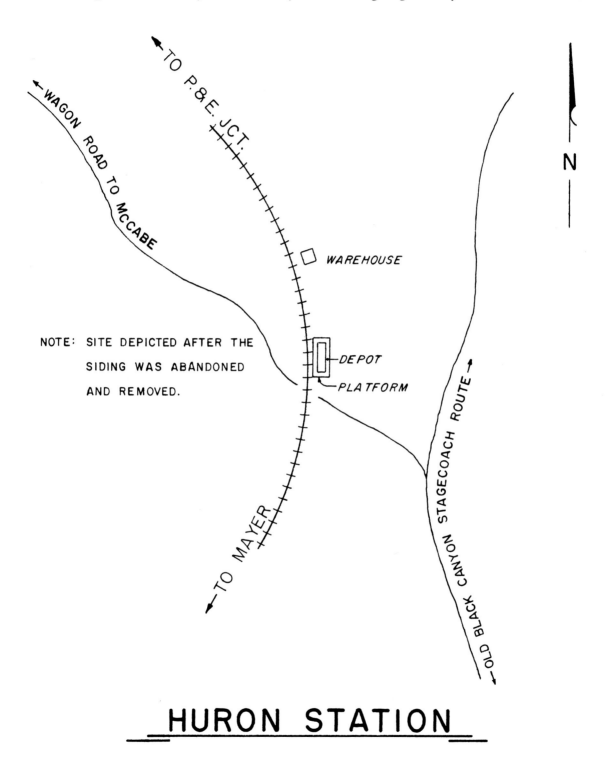

NOTE: SITE DEPICTED AFTER THE SIDING WAS ABANDONED AND REMOVED.

WAGON ROAD TO McCABE

TO P.&E. JCT.

WAREHOUSE

DEPOT

PLATFORM

TO MAYER

OLD BLACK CANYON STAGECOACH ROUTE

N

HURON STATION

SCALE: 1"=200 FEET

MAP BY ROB KROHN

POLAND JUNCTION

1901 - 1939

Frank Murphy originally planned for the branch railroad up Big Bug Creek to join the mainline of the P. & E. at or near Huron. Surveyors and the terrain determined that the junction needed to be farther south than first thought. Poland Junction, as it was aptly named, was established a mile down the rail from Huron and four miles short of Mayer.

There was no mining activity near Poland Junction, but the area saw considerable traffic over the years. The sidetrack at Poland Junction held nineteen cars and was primarily used as a storage yard for empty cars and equipment bound for other destinations. Railroad construction at the location was limited to the railroad track itself and a small utility shed.

The mainline at Poland Junction sliced through a hill, and extensive blasting and grading work was necessary when the line was constructed in 1898. The roadbed and the cut through the hill were widened in 1901 as preparations were made to push the rail toward the upper Big Bug area. A wye, similar to the one at Humboldt, was built just south of the sidetrack. Hundreds of tons of earth were used to construct the roadbed as it started west toward Poland Canyon.

The junction served as a base camp for the construction crews as they graded roadbed and spiked rail on the Poland Branch of the B.M. Ry. The junction was the scene of great enthusiasm and activity as ties, rail, and other construction materials arrived daily. As construction on the branch line progressed westward, the focus of railroad operations and activity also shifted westward. After the branch line was completed in 1902, Poland Junction quieted and was little more than a switchstand, a sidetrack, and a log book.

A tragic mishap occurred at Poland Junction during the early morning hours of an August day in 1902. The northbound train from Mayer pulled two carloads of horses and mules, owned by railroad construction contractors Webster and Edwards, to the sidetrack at Poland Junction. The animals, having seen duty as the right-of-way of the Poland Branch was graded, were headed for Tombstone via Prescott and Phoenix. After leaving the cars on the junction siding, the locomotive steamed toward the high country of Poland Canyon, and dark smoke poured from the black engine stack.

Carried by the summer breeze, a spark from the panting locomotive apparently ignited the roof of one of the wooden livestock cars. The fire spread rapidly through the dry, rough wood and engulfed both cars before it was discovered. Railroad employees ran to the cars and courageously forced open the locked doors. Their heroic efforts freed many mules and horses, but some of the frightened and ornery livestock could not be saved. Nearly half of the forty animals died in the fire or were severely injured and had to be destroyed.

The Arizona Power Company helped establish Poland Junction as a well-known location on the Central Arizona scene. Not only did every southbound train from Prescott pass through the junction, but many mining properties depended on it for electrical power after 1911. The Arizona

Power Company built an electrical relay station at the junction and strung power lines from the location in that year. The power company's interest in the junction increased in 1917 when it established two substations at the site and built a new transmission line into Big Bug country. The new machinery provided power for the numerous mines operated during the latter years of World War I and functioned long after the demise of the mines.

Businesses were never established at Poland Junction, as the only house nearby was that of a cattle rancher, and the need did not exist. The railroad yard and the power substation were essentially Poland Junction. All trains, regardless of direction or destination, stopped at the junction and registered their time and destination in a log book. The log book and yard both experienced fewer entries after World War I ended.

As the mines throughout Big Bug country failed and closed, regularly scheduled service on the Poland Branch was curtailed. Traffic on the line diminished to the extent that trains no longer ran on a schedule, but only as needed to serve the mines that were still being operated. Poland Junction also witnessed considerably less traffic but continued as a storage facility and yard for railroad equipment bound for Mayer and beyond. Abandonment of the Poland Branch Line began in the summer of 1932 and was completed to Poland Junction in April 1939. Part of the northern stem of the wye was retained and served as a short spur for various purposes. Little activity was recorded at Poland Junction after 1939 when the sidetrack was abbreviated into a short spur.

Today, the roadbed of the mainline, sidetrack, and wye is easily seen at Poland Junction. The hundreds of tons of earth that were moved with horse teams, primitive tools, and backbreaking labor and used to construct the roadbed serve as a monument to the fine work of the railroad construction crews. The cut through the hillside is eroded in places, but the engineering work at Poland Junction is still impressive. Several partially buried and rotted ties, twisted and corroded spikes, and rusted tie plates dot the old roadbed. A concrete foundation constructed in 1937 by the Works Progress Administration (WPA)—of unknown purpose—lies crumbled at the junction. A little power substation, now the property of the Arizona Public Service Company, still stands at Poland Junction and relays electrical power to the summer homes and buildings that line Big Bug Creek all the way to Poland Canyon.

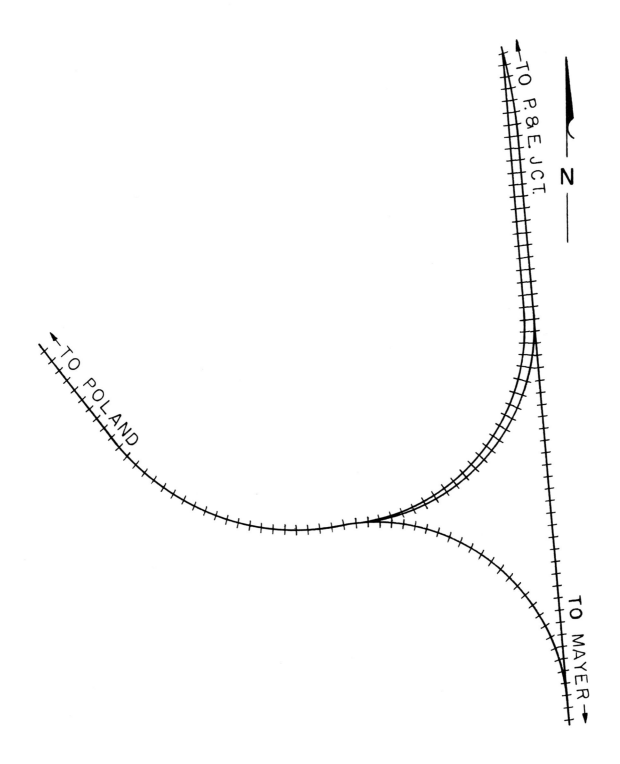

POLAND JUNCTION

As we approach the spur at Arizona City, the baby gauge mining railroad that carries ore from the Hackberry Mine to the old Boggs smelter is visible to the west near Big Bug Creek. The spur at Arizona City is deserted, and the only sign of activity nearby is a flock of birds soaring high over the quiet landscape. Our shrill whistle pierces the air as Mayer appears in the distance and awaits our arrival.

ARIZONA CITY SPUR

1898 - 1958

The Arizona City Spur was named for the small mining community which nestled just west of the railroad mainline to Mayer. The little town was about one-half mile from the rail and near the waters of Big Bug Creek. Established in the late 1880s, Arizona City was originally called Curtis, in honor of the superintendent at the nearby mine. The community served the local miners and the men that operated a small smelter that processed the ore. The camp was little more than mining company offices, a general merchandise store, a boardinghouse, and a butcher shop, but had a post office from 1891 to 1895. A little baby gauge railroad delivered ore from the mines to a small smelter built a short distance away. This railroad was a visual highlight of railroad travel on the Prescott and Eastern mainline, and passengers and crew alike strained for a view of the tiny engine at work.

The mines near Arizona City produced copper and gold ore, but they were not as extensive or profitable as their developers had hoped. The properties were owned by the Commercial Mining Company, a subsidiary of Phelps Dodge. James Douglas, one of the patriarchs of Arizona copper mining, made several visits to Arizona City before his company pulled out of the mines near that community in 1895.

The area was revived briefly in 1899, when Henry B. Clifford fraudulently promoted the mines and the townsite, and again from 1904 to 1909, when the Treadwell Mining Company sporadically operated the mines. The bottom quickly fell out of Clifford's scam, but his name for

the area, Arizona City, had a ring to it and took hold. The Treadwell Company operated the mines until 1909 when several men died in a fire that gutted one of the shafts. The mines closed, and the mining company fell into bankruptcy. The buildings at Arizona City were deserted and disappeared shortly after the mines closed in 1909. The wooden headframes decayed, and only ghosts walked the mine tunnels for nearly twenty years.

The railroad spur at Arizona City witnessed very little traffic over its years of operation. The spur, which was midway between the Black Canyon Road to the east and the tree-lined banks of Big Bug Creek to the west, held two cars and had its switch on the Mayer end of the mainline. The only railroad structure at the location was a solitary utility shed that stood near the spur. Ore was shipped from the spur with some regularity prior to 1909; shipments were sporadic after that year. More often than not, the spur was empty and served as "sunning" ground for the local reptile population. The spur was silent long before the old P. & E. mainline retreated to the Iron King Mine in 1958.

Today, nothing remains at the railroad spur except part of the old roadbed and scattered, rusted railroad spikes. In the distance, toward Big Bug Creek, remnants of the baby gauge railroad grade can be seen in places. Arizona City was reclaimed by mother nature decades ago, and only the rustling of leaves in trees along Big Bug Creek and wildlife that scrambles over mining waste dumps on the pleasantry green landscape break the silence that envelops the area.

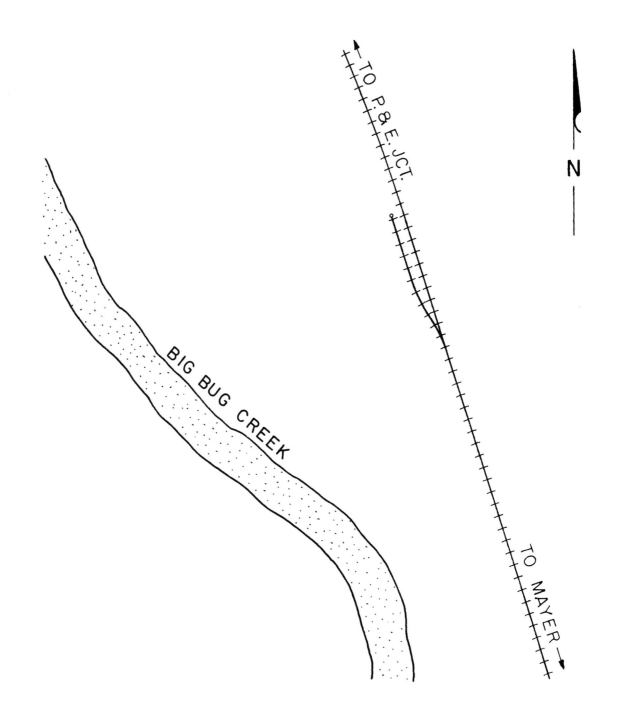

TO P. & E. JCT.

BIG BUG CREEK

TO MAYER

N

ARIZONA CITY SPUR

SCALE: 1" = 200 FEET

MAP BY ROB KROHN

We cross Big Bug Creek and approach the bustling little town of Mayer, the terminus of the Prescott and Eastern Railway and the beginning of the Bradshaw Mountain Railway. The community is a fine example of what can be accomplished in a brief period of time by hard work, foresight, and good fortune. We pass the white two-story hotel and approach the depot. Alongside the depot, the wooden water tank slowly drips, forming a small puddle, as we take on water for the long, hard climb to Crown King. Beyond and to the right of the depot, the business buildings of Mayer cluster along Main Street and invite customers inside. As we look around town, it is hard to believe that a few short years ago all that was here was the stage station of Joe Mayer.

MAYER STATION

1898 - 1958

The early history of Mayer dates to the late 1870s, when a stage station called Big Bug was established near the present-day community. The Big Bug Stage Station should not be confused with the community by that name, which was about eight miles to the northwest. The station was on the Black Canyon Stage Line between Phoenix and Prescott and served as a departure point for the freight teams into the Bradshaw Mountains. Although stage traffic increased as mines and Prescott developed and grew, the stage station was little more than a change-point for horses until Joe Mayer arrived on the scene in 1881.

Mayer arrived in the mountains south of Prescott in 1879 after working in Silver City, New Mexico, and McMillan, near Globe, Arizona. Mayer's first home in the Bradshaw Mountains was in the silver camp, Tip Top. He operated a popular restaurant there until the mines started to play out in 1881. He sold his business in Tip Top, then bought and put his heart and future into the Big Bug Stage Station.

Mayer and his young wife loved the beauty of the area. The sounds of water gurgling playfully in nearby Big Bug Creek and of cottonwood leaves gently quaking in the warm summer breeze drifted toward the stage station. In the spring, the surrounding countryside exploded in magnificent displays of wildflowers and green grass. The commercial possibilities of the location also attracted the attention of Joe Mayer.

A proven entrepreneur, he built a new stage building, house, general store, and saloon along the creek. Around the new buildinigs he planted cherry, black walnut, plum, apple, and other fruit trees. Although annoyed by floods, bandits, and other adversities, Mayer and his stage station prospered. A post office, named Mayer, was established in the Mayer home in 1884, and Joe Mayer's wife, Sarah, was named postmistress.

The growth of Mayer, as the stage station was called after Joe Mayer arrived there in 1881, continued through the early 1890s. A road was graded from Mayer to Crown King and carried freight to and from mines near that community. Mayer served as one of the jump-off points for shipments into the heartland of the Bradshaw Mountains. Freight shipments from near Mayer were not limited to mining equipment and wagons of ore. A deposit of high quality onyx was discovered near the community in 1889, and the stone was cut into large blocks and shipped to Prescott. Mayer, small as it was, was already a key shipping point before the railroad arrived, but its

This photograph, taken in 1930, shows a "doubleheader" taking on water at Mayer and preparing to head back toward Prescott. *Courtesy Blaine Bowman.*

importance as a shipping and distribution center increased dramatically in the fall of 1898.

After several weeks of grading roadbed and laying rail, the Prescott and Eastern Railway reached Mayer on a cold blustery day in October 1898. The railway built several structures in the community that served mining and business interests. One of the first railway buildings completed in town was the sixty-four by twenty foot depot. Surrounded by a wooden freight platform, the building was thoroughly modern for the day, being equipped with both electricity and running water. A short distance from the depot, a water tank was constructed from which the locomotive boilers were filled. The tank was the standard twenty-four foot diameter wooden design used on the P. & E. Ry. and Bradshaw Mountain Lines. Among the other railroad buildings in town were warehouses, a section house, section workers' bunkhouse, tool house, and assorted sheds and loading platforms. The railroad structures at Mayer were served by a long sidetrack that cut behind the depot and warehouses and held forty-two cars.

Following the arrival of the Prescott and Eastern Railway and with Joe Mayer in charge, the town of Mayer experienced five years of rapid growth. The hotel and restaurant of Joe Mayer were relatively close to the depot and provided excellent food and lodging for the railroad excursionists. Although not as well-known as Fred Harvey facilities, from all reports the accommodations at Mayer compared quite favorably with the best in the state. The general mercantile of Joe Mayer was flooded with large orders for everything from dry goods to mining supplies and patent medicines. When construction started on the two branches of the Bradshaw Mountain Railway in 1902, the outlook for Mayer could not have been better.

The main street of town was graded in December 1902, and contractors worked on a number of new buildings. The Joe Mayer block, which was across the street and a little south of his older buildings, was started in 1902. Completed less than a year later, the brick block consisted of four buildings and housed a saloon, restaurant, general store, and barbershop. The store was the showpiece of the block, as the front was dominated by plate glass, and a large gallery extended from three sides of the building. Other merchants were anxious to open stores in the community, but Joe Mayer wisely waited until he was well-established before he sold any land to his competitors.

In 1904, Joe Mayer and two partners incorporated the town of Mayer and sold lots in the community. The 160-acre townsite was divided into business and residential lots that sold for $100 to $500 each. The choice lots measured 40 by 125 feet feet and were along Main Street near the railroad tracks. Property in Mayer sold very well, and it was breathtaking how quickly the business and residential districts developed.

The business district was well-established by 1907, and although new businesses were opened after that time, the days of frenzied real estate dealing were over. The first businesses established in town, excluding the post office and early enterprises of Joe Mayer that dated to the early 1880s, were the Western Union telegraph office in the railway depot and the Wells Fargo office in the

The Mayer Depot and water tank were only a short distance from the business district. This photograph was taken circa 1918. *Courtesy Hattie Marshall.*

same building. The population of about six hundred people quickly supported an assortment of mining company offices, stores, restaurants, hotels, and livery stables. A doctor's office, hospital, and cemetery handled the health problems that arose in the community. The local justice-of-the-peace and the Presbyterian Church provided legal and religious guidance to residents.

Several public utilities were represented in Mayer. Early telephone service to Mayer and nearby communities was furnished by the Prescott Electric Company. Several of Mayer's buildings were equipped with generators and electricity by 1905. Commercial electrical power reached the community in 1909 and was provided by the Arizona Power Company. A water company, later called the Mayer Waterworks, was founded in 1902 by Joe Mayer and his associates. Big Bug Creek at Mayer was not a reliable source of water, as it was often dry or tainted. The company solved the town's water problems with an eight mile pipeline from Crystal Springs. The pipeline delivered 400,000 gallons of pure, clear water each day and allowed the towns growth to continue.

The school district in Mayer was created in the 1880s. It was a one-room schoolhouse constructed near the old buildings of Joe Mayer. In 1897, the enrollment had grown to nine students, and the school was soon relocated. Joe Mayer graciously donated land on a hill overlooking the north end of town. The new schoolhouse was outgrown within two decades, and larger facilities were again needed. The demands were met when a large brick schoolhouse was built on the site in 1916; it housed the halls of higher learning. The schoolhouse, as in many small communities, was the polling place in Mayer for the general elections. As early as 1906, 142 votes were cast in the Mayer Voting Precinct. That figure is more impressive when it is realized that voting privileges were not obtained by women in Arizona until 1912.

Mayer had its own telephone switchboard, and the operator kept many local residents abreast of local news items, but efforts were made to establish a more comprehensive source of news. The first Mayer newspaper, the *Weekly Reflex*, was published briefly in 1898. The *Mayer Miner* and *Big Bug Copper News* were also published in Mayer, but

63

The 1907 class photograph of the one-room Mayer Public School shows everyone in their nicest clothes. *Courtesy Hattie Marshall.*

The P. & E. mainline is in the foreground and the "new" Mayer schoolhouse sits on the hill. This photograph was taken circa 1916. *Courtesy Hattie Marshall.*

both were short-lived. Competition from Prescott papers, the relatively small population of Mayer, and the great expense of publishing a newspaper all contributed to the demise of Mayer's journalistic endeavors.

Even in its hectic early days, Mayer was a peaceful town known for its civic minded townsfolk. That reputation was tarnished somewhat on 18 November 1904 when a tragic shooting death occurred in town. An argument started over a game of cards in a saloon. The opinion of an impartial referee was solicited to settle the dispute. The referee supported the contention of one of the players, and the other stormed out of the bar in a rage. When the referee and a few other men left the bar a short time later, they were confronted on the street by the disgruntled player and fired upon. The first bullet missed its mark entirely, the second struck an onlooker in the foot, and the third lodged in the referee's stomach and proved fatal. The mood of the crowd that gathered turned ugly, and shouts for a lynching were heard. The mob dispersed only after it was learned that the assailant had escaped town and was headed for Mexico.

The siding behind the depot was not the only railroad track at or near Mayer. About one-half mile north of the depot, the railway constructed a wye. Built in the shape of a letter "Y," this layout was not nearly the size of the wyes at Humboldt, Poland Junction, or Crown King but served the same purpose as it allowed locomotives to change direction without a turntable and without uncoupling cars. Unlike Humboldt and Crown King, buildings and loading ramps were not constructed along this wye but were built near the depot in "downtown" Mayer. Beyond the wye, a short distance to the north of town, was the Rigby Spur. This spur was privately owned and maintained by the mining company it served. The Rigby Reduction Company plant was on the slope above Big Bug Creek. The company processed ore for a few years but fell prey to the large ore processing plant at Humboldt. The buildings and machinery at the plant were salvaged and removed.

On the extreme other end of town, about one-

The Rigby Reduction Works is the large structure in the left foreground and Mayer is spread out along the railroad tracks in the distance to the right. *Courtesy Arizona Historical Foundation, Hayden Library, Arizona State University.*

This panoramic view of Mayer was taken in 1907. In this view, looking southeast toward town, the schoolhouse with flagpole and the hotel are in the center of the scene; the railway water tank, depot, and warehouses are visible beyond the schoolhouse; and the Treadwell smelter appears in the distance. *Courtesy Hattie Marshall.*

half mile south of the depot, was the Treadwell Spur. Like the Rigby Spur, it was not railroad property, but was owned by a mining company. The Treadwell Mining Company operated a smelter and several nearby mines, including the Hackberry, Boggs, and Iron Queen. The smelter was completed in 1905 but proved ineffective and did not compete well with the huge Humboldt plant for efficiency or cost. The Treadwell smelter later rebuilt and called the Great Western smelter, was operated intermittently for a few years and then was dismantled.

Maintenance of the tracks and railway facilities near Mayer required a crew of several men. The area served by the Mayer crew was bounded by Huron Station on the north and Turkey Creek Spur on the south. Like similar crews in Humboldt, Middelton, Crown King, Poland, and Prescott and Eastern Junction, the Mayer crew did a commendable job of maintaining long sections of rail. The hard-working railroad men were housed in a dormitory-style bunkhouse near the south end of that community and kept the rails safe for many years.

In the early days after the completion of the P. & E. Ry., Mayer was the railhead, and many shipments originated or terminated in that community. Mining supplies and freight flowed in and out of the Mayer depot with impressive regularity. The shipments from Mayer fell off after the two branch lines were completed, but traffic on the tracks through the community was greater than ever before. Shipments of ore and mining supplies rode the rail through town, but shipments from the community itself were mainly livestock. Some goats and cattle were loaded at Mayer, but the livestock shipments were primarily sheep. In the early days of the P. & E. Ry., the sheep grazed along the mainline near the depot. In later years, the sheep were loaded south of town at the Gray Eagle Spur and at Cordes Siding. Sheep shipments, although seasonal, remained large and numerous for many years.

Joe Mayer accomplished a great deal in his town before he died on a drizzly day in December 1909. The Bradshaw Mountain entrepreneur was felled when his gun accidentally discharged as he lost his footing while investigating noises outside his

This photograph of the P. & E. Railway depot in Mayer was taken circa 1900. The sheep grazed along the mainline and awaited shipment to the meat processing centers of the Midwest. *Courtesy Arizona Historical Foundation, Hayden Library, Arizona State University.*

home. At the time of his death, Mayer was one of the most progressive towns in Central Arizona. Joe Mayer funded the town's water system, donated the land and several hundred dollars for the schoolhouse and school books, contributed large sums of money to charities, and never turned his back on a man who needed a loan or a handout. After Joe Mayer's death, his philosophy of "help thy neighbor" was carried on by his many friends, neighbors, and relatives in Mayer. Joe Mayer's business fortunes suffered for his generosity, but his legacy of kindness and benevolence was known the state over.

Activity in Mayer slowed during the national depression of 1907 and remained languid until the onset of World War I. A large number of railway ore cars from the De Soto and Blue Bell Mines went through Mayer on their way to the Humboldt smelter during World War I, but Mayer itself did not benefit from the resurgence of the mining industry as much as was expected. Some miners employed at nearby mines resided in Mayer and spent their wages there, but few new construction or expansion projects were funded in Mayer. The community was alive again with freight and ore shipments through town, but the days of unbridled growth and optimism in Mayer were more than a decade in the past.

In most respects, Mayer remained relatively unchanged during World War I. The population rose slightly to just over six hundred as miners and smelter workers lived in Mayer and commuted to their work in nearby mines and at Humboldt. They helped the local economy during their stay in town, but few stayed after the mines closed. Ranching, along with some local mining, remained the mainstay of the Mayer economy. The Mayer Hotel, White House Hotel, and the Owl Movie Theatre were popular spots in town, and local folks still gathered there on Saturday nights to discuss the week's news. Some other local landmarks did not fare as well. The Mayer Hospital, which overlooked town from its perch on the hill south of the community, was closed and became a private residence. Seriously ill patients were cared for in hospitals at Humboldt and Prescott. Another casualty of the 1920s was the Mayer State Bank. The bank emptied its cash drawers, pulled its shades, and locked its doors for the last time. Several other Mayer businesses cut back on services and inventory during the depression, but the community weathered the economic storm relatively well.

The next three decades of Mayer were characterized by a lack of development. Copper ore was mined from the Blue Bell and a few other mines nearby, but Mayer received little direct benefit. The population of the community grew about 25 percent during World War II when mining activity increased, but the miners left town shortly after the war ended, and the mines closed. Mayer slowly became a community of retirees and summer homes. Many of the historic buildings in town were not maintained and fell into disrepair.

As the volume of traffic over the railway diminished, the railway buildings in Mayer deteriorated at the hands of vandals and the ravages of time. Several of the weathered railway buildings were razed, and a few others were moved from the community. The passenger depot was privately purchased and moved to Phoenix, where it became part of a collection of railroad memorabilia. One of the old storage buildings was acquired by a small railroad museum, "Bowman's Diggins," and moved just south of town. The railway abandoned its right-of-way through Mayer and removed its rail in 1958. When possible, the railway returned its land in Mayer to its original owners or their heirs.* Almost six acres of land in the community were donated to the town of Mayer. The Mayer Chamber of Commerce and other local organizations raised funds and built a community center on the land. The center provides programs for youngsters, the aged, and civic groups. The legacy of Joe Mayer still lives in the community that bears his name.

A few of the old buildings remain, but today the town is a shadow of its former self. The brick schoolhouse was closed in 1982 but still stands above town and keeps a watchful eye on the

*The railroad agreed at the time the right-of-way was acquired that, if the right-of-way was ever abandoned, the land was to be returned to its original owners. This was a common railroad practice and applied to the entire length of the P. & E. and B.M. Ry. lines.

The Mayer Hospital is shown circa 1920 after it had become a private residence. *Courtesy Hattie Marshall.*

The Mayer Depot and water tank serve a "doubleheader" with four ore cars in tow. The cars were bound for the Humboldt smelter. *Courtesy Blaine Bowman.*

railroad roadbed. The building is currently used for storage of school district property. The stately Mayer Hotel, built in 1889 by Joe Mayer, is currently being preserved. The White House Hotel, Mayer State Bank building, and a few other landmarks have survived. The old roadbed is still visible as it enters and leaves town, but paving and roadwork in the community have erased all signs of the right-of-way within the town. Along highway 69 south of Mayer, the smokestack of a long vanished smelter stands on a hill and hints at the industry of yesteryear. Mayer, although not a ghost town in the truest sense, has a colorful past rich in mining and railroad history and deserves more attention than a hasty drive through town.

SANTA FE, PRESCOTT AND PHX. RY.

TO ASH FORK

PRESCOTT & EASTERN RY.

N

TO PHOENIX

PRESCOTT

WHIPPLE

YAEGER

PRESCOTT AND
EASTERN JCT.

CHERRY CREEK

HUMBOLDT

IRON KING

POLAND BRANCH
OF THE B.M. RY.

CHAPARRAL

HENRIETTA

HURON

PROVIDENCE

EUGENIE

POLAND JCT.

POLAND

BLOCK

ARIZONA CITY

MAYER

GRAY EAGLE

BLUE BELL

CORDES

CROWN KING BRANCH OF THE
BRADSHAW MOUNTAIN OF THE RY.

TURKEY CREEK

MIDDELTON

PECK

SADDLE

HORSE THIEF

CROWN KING

SCALE: 1"= 6 MILES

MAP BY ROB KROHN

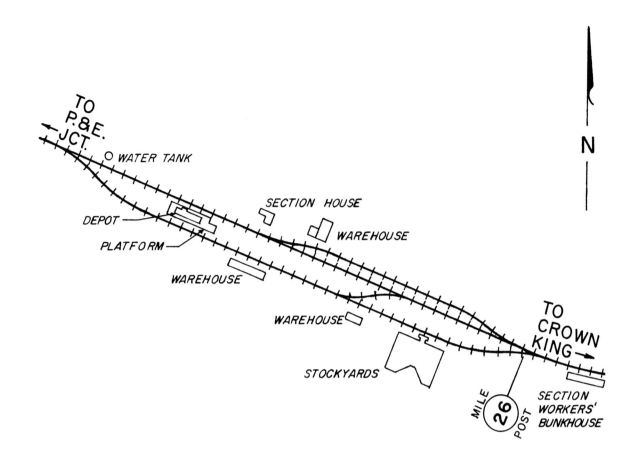

TO
P.&E.
JCT.

WATER TANK

N

SECTION HOUSE

DEPOT

PLATFORM

WAREHOUSE

WAREHOUSE

WAREHOUSE

TO
CROWN
KING

STOCKYARDS

MILE
26
POST

SECTION
WORKERS'
BUNKHOUSE

MAYER STATION

SCALE: 1"=250 FEET

MAP BY ROB KROHN

As we leave Mayer, the morning sun smiles on the green Bradshaw foothills, and the landscape is accented by the color of spring flowers. Just over the grassy knoll from Mayer proper is the Gray Eagle Spur. The spur is little more than a flagstop and appears deserted as we roll by.

GRAY EAGLE SPUR

1915 - 1958

The Gray Eagle Spur was named for and served the Gray Eagle Reduction Works. In April 1915, during the frenzied mining activity that accompanied World War I, the reduction works and spur were constructed less than a mile south of the Mayer depot. The spur was east of the mainline, had its connection on the north end of the spur, and was just over seven hundred feet in length. A little storage shed and small loading platform alongside the spur were the only railroad-owned structures at the site. The reduction plant closed in 1917, and after less than three full years of operation, the facility and the Gray Eagle Spur were rendered silent.

Just across the mainline from the Gray Eagle Spur were stockyards, a loading platform, and livestock chutes. These structures, which were just west of the railroad mainline and just east of the old Black Canyon Stage Road, were used by ranchers and also by the seasonal sheep drives. The stockyards were very busy during the early days of the Bradshaw Mountain Railway, but in 1922 the stockyards at Cordes Siding were rebuilt, and livestock shipping centered at that location. This shift reversed itself in 1939 when the rail was removed from Cordes Siding back to Blue Bell, and ranchers again used the old stockyards near the

Gray Eagle Spur. The residents of Mayer, who had complained only a few years earlier about the smells and other unpleasantries that accompanied the stockyards, were happy to have the cattlemen and their trade back in town after an absence of almost two decades.

The Gray Eagle Reduction Works never saw much traffic on the railroad. The large mill and smelter at Humboldt and smaller plants scattered throughout the Bradshaw Mountain mining country captured the lion's share of the ore processing business. The Gray Eagle facility operated only briefly and did not have much of an impact on the area. The spur that served the reduction plant was shortened in 1928 from 700 to 389 feet and was used as a storage yard for railroad equipment. The spur and mainline were removed in 1958 when the highway of steel retreated to the Iron King Spur.

Mayer has grown over the years, and today the sites of the Gray Eagle Spur and the stockyards are within the city limits of that community. Gas stations, restaurants, mobile home dealerships, and ranch houses have devoured the land that was once the outskirts of Mayer. Nothing remains at the site of the Gray Eagle Spur or the old stockyards.

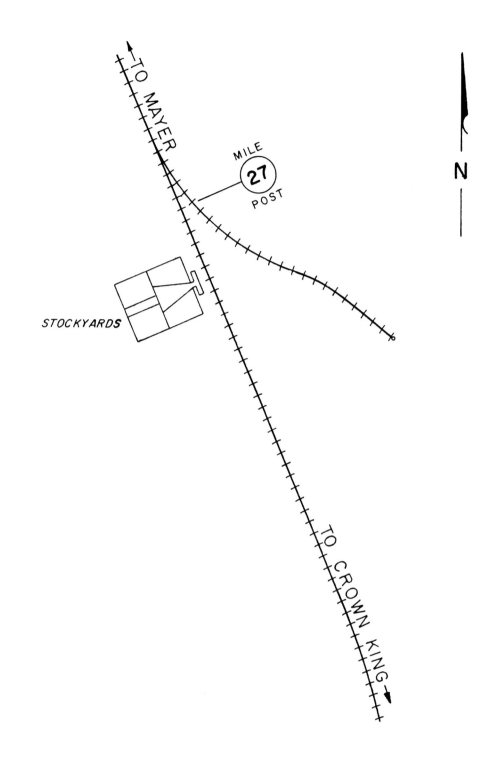

N

TO MAYER

MILE
(27)
POST

STOCKYARDS

TO CROWN KING

GRAY EAGLE SPUR

SCALE: 1"= 200 FEET

MAP BY ROB KROHN

BLUE BELL SIDING

1906 - 1958

Just over two miles southeast of Mayer, in the brush-covered Bradshaw foothills, was Blue Bell Siding. The siding primarily served the Blue Bell Mine, which was located in rough mountain country six miles south of Mayer. The siding was not part of the original Bradshaw Mountain Railway System, but its construction in February 1906 hastened the development of the Blue Bell Mine. The Blue Bell Mine produced over $14,000,000 in copper ore and was second only to the Iron King as the richest mine in the Bradshaw Range.

The Blue Bell Mine, like many of the Bradshaw's richest properties, was not one of the area's earliest discoveries. The Blue Belle and two adjacent claims were filed in January 1893 and were collectively known as the Blue Belle Mine. The claims were amended to ensure clear title in 1899, and the "e" was droped from Belle. The early operation of the mine was limited by rudimentary equipment and lack of capital. The ore was exceptionally rich. It averaged over 15 percent copper and significant amounts of gold and silver, but because of financial shortcomings only 400 tons of ore were mined from the time of discovery through May 1899.

The location of the mine and the richness of the ore made the property ideal for far greater activity and production. The arrival of the railroad in Mayer in 1898 and the construction of the Valverde smelter in 1899 made large-scale investment and production at the mine financially possible. Investment capital was obtained, and the mine was outfitted with heavy machinery. Production increased dramatically only to be quickly halted by a complicated lawsuit among the owners of the mine. The property was idle through 1905.

The Blue Bell property was modernized and reopened in late 1905 when it was acquired by the Consolidated Arizona Smelting Company (C.A.S.). This company made the financial commitment that was necessary to develop the mine to its potential. New hoisting machinery capable of accommodating deep mining operations was installed. Modern pumps, drills, and compressors were also purchased and put to use at the mine. The company also built an aerial tramway from the mine to a location near the Bradshaw Mountain Railway mainline a short distance south of Mayer. This tramway was designed by the same company that constructed the tram at the De Soto Mine near Middelton in 1904. The tramways were similar in many respects, but the Blue Bell tramway was four miles in length, which was considerably longer than the one used at the De Soto, and unlike its counterpart, the Blue Bell tram was powered by powerful gasoline engines. The gigantic wooden and iron tramway terminal stood a few hundred feet from the mainline of the Bradshaw Mountain Railway to Crown King.

The Consolidated Arizona Smelting Company approached the Bradshaw Mountain Railway and requested a spur line be built from the mainline to the site of the tramway terminal. It should be noted that Frank M. Murphy and the Santa Fe Railway held large amounts of stock in C.A.S. The B.M. Ry, decided, not surprisingly, it needed a siding at the

This photograph, taken circa 1908, shows the imposing tramway terminal at Blue Bell Siding. *Courtesy Charles Nichols.*

location, and in February 1906 a sidetrack was completed that served the Blue Bell tramway facility. This siding ran alongside the terminal and was capable of holding eighteen ore cars. The construction of this siding proved to be an excellent business move, as the revenues from the ore shipments paid for it many times over.

The railroad siding, in addition to benefiting the mining company and the railway, was of great importance to the Arizona Power Company. This company was established to meet the electricity demands of Central Arizona. The company constructed several power plants throughout the area it served. One of the power plants was a short distance from Blue Bell Siding. In May 1908, the power company graded a road and built a telephone line from Blue Bell Siding to the site of its proposed plant near the mouth of Fossil Creek. More than three hundred men were employed to transport the electrical machinery from Blue Bell Siding to the construction site. In 1909, the power company started the sale of electrical power to Prescott, Mayer, Jerome, Cottonwood, and many of the Bradshaw Mountain mines. For several weeks, Blue Bell Siding served as the temporary headquarters of the power company's construction crews. After the plant was completed, the construction workers were assigned to projects elsewhere, but heavy machinery and supplies destined for the power plant were received at Blue Bell Siding many times over the years.

The Consolidated Arizona Smelting Company built a camp at the mine site for its miners and also

constructed a small camp at the railroad siding for the men who operated the tramway. The buildings at the mine were the combination office building-cookhouse-superintendent's quarters, bunkhouse, upper tramway terminal, hoist building, change room, combination store and pool hall, and three residential dwellings. The peak population at this camp was about 125 people but was usually much smaller. At the railroad siding, the camp was much less extensive. A warehouse, tool house, bunkhouse-cookhouse, and four residential dwellings, all owned by C.A.S., comprised the camp. This little community was known as Blue Bell, and its population averaged twenty-five people. A crude, rocky road led from the siding to the mine and was used extensively by miners who sought entertainment in Mayer.

Life at the siding was far from luxurious. The camp was owned by the mining company, and the residents were all C.A.S. employees or their families. Bunkhouse and cookhouse accommodations were provided and cost one dollar a day for the single men and slightly more for the men with families. The camp was equipped with a telephone and enjoyed the convenience of electric lights by 1909. Medical treatment beyond first aid was not available at either Blue Bell camp, but a company hospital was maintained for C.A.S. employees near the company smelter in Humboldt.

The Blue Bell camps offered little recreation for their residents. Cards, billiards, and hunting were the common forms of entertainment. The two camps combined and formed a baseball team when

This 1906 photograph of Upper Blue Bell Camp shows many of the early buildings and the tramway that led to the railroad siding. *Courtesy Sharlot Hall Museum.*

baseball fever swept through the Arizona Territory in 1906. The Blue Bell team did respectably against the Humboldt "Smoke-Eaters," "Salt River Nine," and teams from Mayer, McCabe, Prescott, and Jerome. A saloon never existed at either Blue Bell property, but the most active years of the Blue Bell Mine and camps were during prohibition, and liquor was not legally available except for "medicinal purposes." The Blue Bell camps, particularly the camp at Blue Bell Siding, had close ties with the nearby town of Mayer.

Mayer provided the Blue Bell camps with much more than friendly competition on the baseball field. A business sector never developed at Blue Bell Siding, and essential goods and services for both Blue Bell camps were provided by Mayer. Blue Bell residents relied upon the post office, Wells Fargo, and mercantile services of their neighboring community. Mayer merchants benefited from and enjoyed the trade of Blue Bell residents as foodstuffs, clothing, and drug supplies were usually purchased from their stores. The Yavapai

County County Sheriff stationed in Mayer maintained law and order at the Blue Bell camps, but his visits were usually social ones as C.A.S. did not tolerate lawlessness among its men. Voting was taken seriously in the Blue Bell camps, and the men were well-informed and active politically. The Blue Bell Mine had its own voting precinct in 1902 and again from 1920 through 1924, but during most years the residents at the mine joined the residents of Blue Bell Siding and voted in Mayer. The youngsters at Blue Bell Siding also had close ties to Mayer, as they attended school there. A small school was active at the Blue Bell Mine intermittently from 1906 through 1916, after which students at the mine were transported to the schoolhouse in Mayer.

Water for both Blue Bell camps was also supplied by Mayer. A pipeline was constructed from Mayer to Blue Bell Siding and provided water for that trackside community. Drinking water at the mine site was always in great demand but was very scarce. The 150,000 gallons of water that were pumped out of the mine daily were used for mining purposes, but this water was not fit to drink. The water shortage at the mine was solved to a large extent with water from Blue Bell Siding. Drinking water was placed in special containers at Blue Bell Siding and shipped to the mine on the tramway.

Occasionally, shipments of supplies on the aerial tramway from Blue Bell Siding to the mine did not reach their destination. The tramway was an impressive piece of machinery, but not without a few problems. The system operated most efficiently when ore buckets were spaced at equal intervals along the cable. If ore production was not sufficient to sustain operation of the tram, waste rock was loaded in the buckets at the mine and dumped behind the tramway terminal at the siding. The extra weight kept the system operating smoothly but produced increased wear and tear on the system. As years passed, increasing numbers of buckets fell from the cable and crashed to the landscape below. An alarmed tram operator jumped for cover when he witnessed one such incident. A clutch device malfunctioned on an empty ore bucket returning to the mine site, and the bucket rolled backwards down the cable out of control. This mishap would not have been the cause of serious concern except that the bucket following the "runaway" carried four boxes of dynamite. The collision of the buckets knocked both free of the cable, and they fell to the hillside below. The dynamite was scattered over the entire hillside but fortunately did not explode. The same hillsides saw numerous buckets pass overhead during the years of great activity at the Blue Bell Mine, but serious accidents were few.

The railroad never constructed a depot or any other buildings at Blue Bell Siding. Although there was a great deal of freight activity to and from the siding, there was minimal passenger traffic at that location. There really wasn't enough passenger traffic on the entire Prescott and Eastern Railway and the Bradshaw Mountain lines to pay any but the smallest bills. Most local residents, even in the large communities of Crown King, Poland, Mayer, and Humboldt, rode their horses or buggies to other communities. The railroad was primarily used by high ranking mining officials and for freight and ore shipments. The outskirts of Mayer were less than a mile from Blue Bell Siding, and railroad facilities there made construction of similar structures at the siding unnecessary.

World War I was the most active period in the life of Blue Bell Siding as enormous quantities of ore were mined at the Blue Bell property during those years. The equipment at the mine was operated at capacity and over four hundred tons of ore were

mined and shipped from the railroad siding daily. It may be remembered that four hundred tons was the same figure mined during the first seven years at the Blue Bell Mine combined. Blue Bell Siding was the scene of bustling activity as hopper-bottom ore cars lined the siding and mining supplies and freight arrived daily. The tramway was operated almost sixteen hours each day, and its cables sang in the crisp clear air.

The production figures of the war years at the Blue Bell Mine made Blue Bell Siding one of the largest revenue producers on the Bradshaw Mountain Railway and Prescott and Eastern Line. The other locations that were dependable revenue producers were Middelton, Humboldt, and, in later years, Iron King. Although shipments were placed and received at various points along the lines, few stations supported their maintenance after about 1912.

The economic downswing of the metals market and the collapse of the parent company clouded the future of the Blue Bell Mine, forcing it to close as the sun set on 1921. The impact at the siding was immediate. Without the shipments to and from the Blue Bell Mine, the siding was deserted except for a watchman. Little maintenance work was done, and the tramway and nearby structures began to show the effects of the elements and time. Consolidated Arizona Smelting Company was reorganized as the Southwest Metals Company in 1922, and the Blue Bell Mine was reopened. Although operating once again, activity at the mine was on a much smaller scale than in the "golden years" of World War I. Railroad service at the siding was cut to three days per week and did not need to be as often as that. The railroad siding was shortened into a spur and yearned to see more traffic.

Activity at the mine and subsequently at Blue Bell Siding slowed further over the next several years. The removal of the non-essential equipment for salvage and resale began at the Blue Bell Mine in 1924. The mine yielded small amounts of copper ore through 1926 when it closed. The buildings at the mine site were removed, as they were costly to maintain and were not necessary should the mine be leased to a local mining company. The mine was leased from 1927 to 1931, and some ore was shipped from the siding, but neglect, deterioration, and high weeds marked Blue Bell Siding and the once imposing tramway terminal. The tramway was badly in need of repair and rapidly became not only too costly for a small local company to operate but also too dangerous. It took several weeks to salvage the proud old tram, but the last of the wire cable and massive timbers was hauled away to the scrap pile in 1932. Trucks that carried the remnants of the tramway sent dust clouds drifting upward as they roared past the rundown railroad siding that only a few years before was perhaps the busiest location on the entire line.

Little activity has occurred at the Blue Bell Mine in the last fifty years. The salvage operations, vandals, and natural elements quickly reduced the community at Blue Bell Siding to two dilapidated dwellings. In 1939, the sidetrack at Blue Bell which had been shortened to a spur seventeen years earlier, was shortened again, and a little loading platform was constructed where the tramway terminal once stood. Some exploration was conducted in the late thirties, and brief activity was witnessed during Work War II, but rumors of rich discoveries and grandiose plans that never materialized characterize the last half-century at the Blue Bell Mine.

Today, little trace remains of the once bustling Blue Bell Siding. The Santa Fe Railway abandoned and removed its track from Blue Bell Siding to the Iron King Mine in 1958. The dwellings at the siding disappeared years ago, and only a waste dump of rock marks the site of the tramway terminal. Brush and wildlife have reclaimed the railroad grade at the siding, no trespassing signs and a flagstone quarry mark the mine site, and little more than memories commemorate the second richest mining operaton in the Bradshaw Mountains.

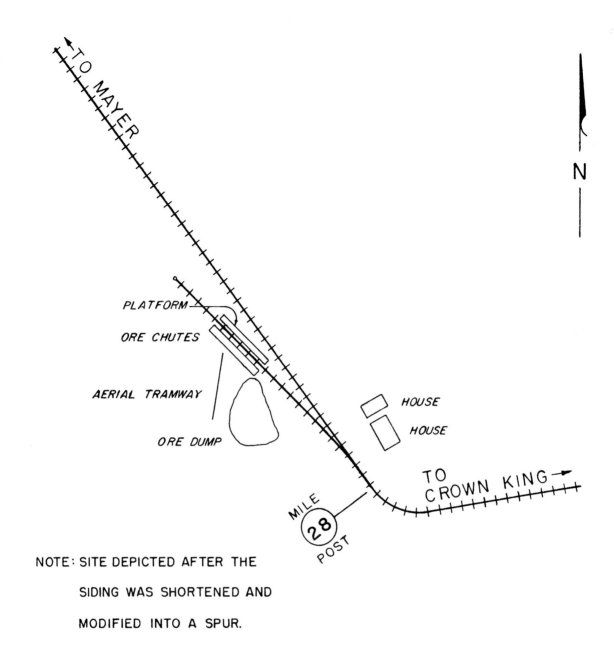

TO MAYER

N

PLATFORM

ORE CHUTES

AERIAL TRAMWAY

ORE DUMP

HOUSE

HOUSE

TO CROWN KING

MILE 28 POST

NOTE: SITE DEPICTED AFTER THE
SIDING WAS SHORTENED AND
MODIFIED INTO A SPUR.

BLUE BELL SIDING

SCALE: 1"= 200 FEET   MAP BY ROB KROHN

The rail turns in a southerly direction below the siding at Blue Bell and heads toward the higher range of the Bradshaws. We cross part of the foothills where only a couple of mines and an occasional prospect hole are seen. The terrain is well-suited to raising livestock; holding pens and corrals appear on the countryside. As we approach Cordes Siding, we see the livestock pen there being used by cowhands branding steers. They tip their hats in response to our shrill whistle, and we steam onward into Cedar Canyon.

CORDES SIDING

1902 - 1939

The community of Cordes, a quarter-of-a-century older than the Bradshaw Mountain Railway, owed its early existence to the Black Canyon Stage Route. The little settlement was founded in 1875 as a stagecoach stop and change-point for horses on the road between Phoenix and Prescott. About thirty miles southeast of Prescott, it was originally called Antelope or Antelope Station after the hill and creek in the area. The station house was purchased by John Henry Cordes in 1883. He arrived in the Bradshaw Mountains in 1875 and worked several years at the Tip Top Mine before entering the stage business at Antelope. Prior to the completion of the Santa Fe, Prescott and Phoenix Railway, the Black Canyon Stage Route was one of the main north-south arteries through the Arizona Territory.

The economy and population of Central Arizona grew tremendously and, as a result, the stage route and Cordes enjoyed much traffic and prosperity. In 1886, Cordes applied to establish a post office in the community. His application was denied under the name Antelope due to a duplication but was approved as Cordes. The community assumed the Cordes name after the post office was officially granted on 9 June 1886. In addition to the stage station and post office, a general merchandise store and saloon were established in the community by John Cordes.

The Santa Fe, Prescott and Phoenix Railway changed the course of transportation through the community. After the railway was completed in 1895, freighting and stage travel over the Black Canyon Route declined dramatically. The railroad was simply quicker, cheaper, and safer. The stage road deteriorated as it witnessed only sporadic traffic. A wise businessman, Cordes developed ties with many neighboring ranchers and operators of nearby mines. The little town soon supplied local ranching and mining operations with a wide range of goods and services.

Like Joe Mayer's community, Cordes was on the sheep trail between Flagstaff and west Phoenix. Although the drives were seasonal, they brought more than wool to the little towns along the way. The sheepherders and their families traveled with the flocks as they moved across the territory. In the autumn, the flocks headed south for the warm climate, and in the spring they headed back to Williams and Flagstaff. For as many as sixty days, twice a year, the sheepmen set up camp near Cordes. The community provided makeshift housing, shearing and dipping facilities, and supplies for the drives. The money and friendship of the nomadic sheep ranchers were warmly received in Cordes.

Prior to the arrival of the Bradshaw Mountain Railway in 1902, mining supplies into that range were shipped over the few good wagon roads that existed. Many mines received their supplies and equipment from Prescott via Cordes. With the exception of a few worthless prospect holes, there was no mining activity in the immediate vicinity of Cordes. However, the Richinbar Mine and numerous other mines a few miles away received supply shipments through the small community.

Wagon roads and direct freight routes were eventually built that served the mines and communities to the west of Cordes, but despite the fact that it was bypassed, the settlement managed to survive.

The community even displayed many of the signs of "permanence." Along with the post office, saloon, and store, the community supported a local school district. In 1897, the one-room schoolhouse was filled with fourteen students. The full-time population of Cordes was twenty-five at the turn of the century. Several of the local residents served as election officers for the general elections; they traveled to the general store at Turkey Creek where they cast their ballots and assumed their civic responsibilities. A shallow well provided plenty of water for the residents, and the deputy sheriff in Mayer provided any law enforcement that was necessary. The saloon and general merchandise store did especially well during the sheep drives and during the construction of the B.M. Ry.

The rail of the B.M. Ry. passed four miles to the west of Cordes. The difficult terrain of Cedar Canyon and the absence of mineral deposits farther east prevented the route from passing through Cordes. The construction through Cedar Canyon was so arduous that several horses died from exhaustion or were injured and had to be shot. A burial ground was established near the canyon for the livestock that gave their lives in the construction of the railroad. The site grew larger by the day as the railroad grade was forced through the rugged countryside.

The Greek and Italian stonemasons on the railroad construction crews spent as much time as possible in Cordes. The men enjoyed playfully teasing the children and bought a great deal of wine and liquor. They drank, danced, and sang until early morning to forget the hazards, hardships, and loneliness of their work. These workers constructed hundreds of retaining walls and drainage boxes without the use of mortar. The craftsmanship of these skilled workers was exceptional and made their talents much sought after.

In 1902, a short siding was laid just north of Cedar Canyon that served the town of Cordes and was named for the community. A livestock yard, warehouse, and loading platform were also constructed at the siding. The original structures were rather modest. However, in 1922, the livestock yard was expanded when loading facilities, scales, and sheep holding pens were moved to the siding from Mayer five miles away.

The completion of the railroad to Crown King brought to a virtual end the shipments of mining supplies from Cordes to the inner canyons of the Bradshaw Mountains. Cordes managed to hang on by supplying local cattle ranchers and the sheep drives. With the decline of shipments through Cordes, it is surprising that the local population increased to fifty by 1907. The town and all of its business enterprises were owned and operated by the Cordes family. As the family grew in size, room additions were made to the old stage station. The store and saloon were housed in the expanded original structure. The Cordes School District was discontinued in 1906, as most of the Cordes children were beyond school age. The younger members of the family resided in Mayer and attended school there during the school year. For all of the advantages that the little town's location on the Black Canyon State Route brought, the community was still somewhat isolated.

The early powerlines into the area were installed at great expense and served only the large mines. Cordes was not near any of those mines or their powerlines. The community did not have power from a public utility until long after most other towns had grown accustomed to the luxury.

A new chapter was written in the history of the little town in 1910. The elder Cordes retired and turned the businesses over to his son. Charles H. Cordes, heir to the community, constructed a new building for the store and saloon. The new structure, like the one it replaced, did not have electricity. The convenience was added circa 1918 when a generator was obtained and the building was wired for lights; powerlines finally reached the community in 1941. With the completion of the new store, the old building was used exclusively by the family as a residence. A fine grand opening celebration was held on the Fourth of July, 1910; people from the surrounding area and friends from as far away as Prescott were on hand to help christen the "modern" building. The "old fashioned" festivities were enjoyed by everyone present and were the talk of the countryside.

Other construction projects soon took shape in Cordes; a barn was built in 1912, and a gas station was opened in 1915. The gas station was one of the first in the area and was built to service the automobiles that were using the Black Canyon Road. The first cars that ventured past Cordes did so circa 1909. The old wagon road up Antelope Hill was a steep stretch not constructed with the tempermental automobile in mind. The first several vehicles that tried to climb the hill had to be helped up the slope by horsepower of the original variety. The current road up Antelope Hill was constructed in 1915 and, coupled with advances in

John H. and Lizzie Cordes, the founders of Cordes, Arizona. *Courtesy Mynne Jarman.*

automobile technology, helped make the Black Canyon Road the scene of great amounts of traffic once again.

Recreation in the community was similar to that in other Bradshaw Mountain towns of the period. The ever-popular reading, singing, dancing, card playing, hunting, and athletic competitions were enjoyed in Cordes. Though isolated in some respects, it was a "one-horse" town with a unique cosmopolitan flavor. Although the community was somewhat isolated in that it received electricity and phone service long after neighboring communities, it was not nearly as remote as might be thought. Travelers on the Black Canyon Road, first in stagecoaches and later in automobiles, kept the residents of Cordes informed of the latest news. People, attitudes, and styles of all kinds went through Cordes and exposed the townspeople to concepts and ideas from throughout the world.

The increase in vehicle traffic, though renewing life to Cordes, signaled the beginning of the end for Cordes Siding. The siding received minimal use after 1908, being used almost exclusively for sheep and cattle shipments. As trucks became more durable and dependable in the late teens, they replaced the railroad as the prime shipper of livestock from the area. The removal of the rail from Cordes Siding back to Blue Bell Siding in December 1939 did not have much of an impact on the community.

The little community of Cordes continued to do well into the forties. The population was abut twenty in 1942. The saloon was replaced by a drug counter in the general store, but it was the settlement's gas station that kept the town alive. The post office was discontinued in November 1944. The community was bypassed again when the new Black Canyon Highway was constructed two miles east of town.

The Cordes General Store constructed in 1910 burned to the ground in the forties, but much of the original stage station still exists, incorporated within the walls of the old house. The gas station, which closed in the seventies, and the weathered barn still watch over the road they served for sixty years. Henry Cordes, grandson of John Henry Cordes, resides in the family house. At the railroad siding, a small corral, sun-bleached concrete foundations, and the railroad grade are all that are visible.

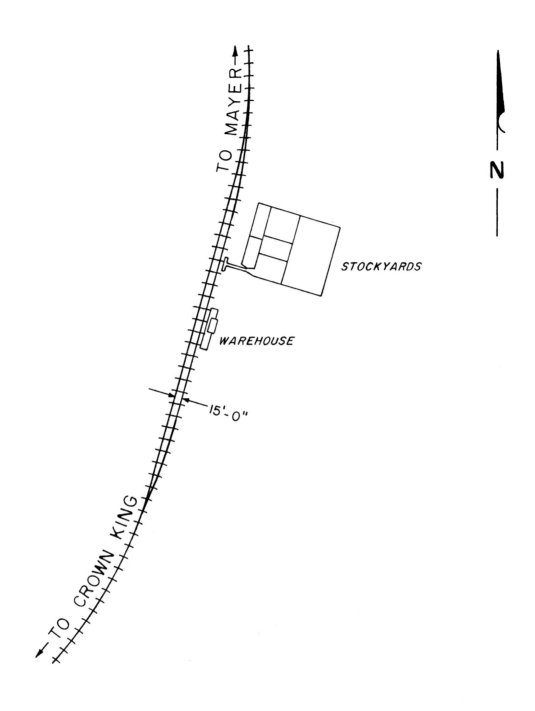

TO MAYER→

STOCKYARDS

WAREHOUSE

15'-0"

TO CROWN KING

N

CORDES SIDING

SCALE: 1"=200 FEET   MAP BY ROB KROHN

TURKEY CREEK SPUR

1902 - 1932

Although the Turkey Creek Mining District was created in 1864, it was the mid-1890s before the community by that name was established. Surrounded on all sides by small mines of moderate wealth, the community was founded as a central gathering and supply point for the miners. Turkey Creek found itself on the stage route from Prescott via Crown King in late 1897, but the settlement was not much more than a handful of ramshackle miners' cabins.

When the Prescott and Eastern Railway arrived in Mayer, it spurred local mining activity and the growth of Turkey Creek. A year later, in 1899, the population of the settlement had increased, and a little grade school was in session. The same year, the citizens started efforts to have a post office established in the community. The local mines, once isolated, were now only a few miles from the railhead in Mayer. Orders for large pieces of mining equipment were placed, and more miners were needed.

The route of the Bradshaw Mountain Railway was carefully planned to serve as many mines as possible. Those near Turkey Creek had hardly been tapped by the turn of the century, and the limits of their wealth were still undetermined. Frank Murphy knew his railroad relied heavily upon shipments of supplies and ore for its income. He was well aware of the mutual benefits the mines and the railroad would reap from one another and directed his surveyors to include the promising area on the route of the Bradshaw Mountain Railway. The rail reached Turkey Creek

in 1902 and brought dreams of prosperity to yet another town.

When the railroad construction crews left Mayer in 1902 and started laying rail toward Crown King, they were closely followed by an entrepreneur, Leverett Nellis, who changed the appearance and future of Turkey Creek. Nellis was quick to take advantage of the concentration of labor and capital. He had traveled widely in the Arizona Territory before arriving in Mayer and had started a lumber business there in 1901. He supplied many of the materials for construction projects in Mayer, McCabe, and Poland, but saw greater opportunity in the railroad. He carefully studied the construction route and observed that Turkey Creek was one of the busiest points along the right-of-way. Mines near the community ordered mining equipment like never before. One freight team after another left the railroad spur at Turkey Creek and headed to mines in the neighboring hills. For several weeks the town was also a base camp for the railroad construction crews as they laid rail to Middelton.

Nellis purchased land in Turkey Creek and opened a general store, saloon, restaurant, freighting business, and cattle ranch. He also renewed and intensified the efforts to have a post office granted to the community. His efforts were rewarded in March 1903 when the post office request was approved and Nellis was named postmaster. Not surprisingly, the post office was in the corner of his general store, which didn't hurt his business any. The post office was named

In this early photograph of Turkey Creek, the original Nellis General Store is the large false front building in the left center. When James Cleator constructed his new store building a few years later it was along the railroad grade just out of view to the right. *Courtesy Nell Nellis Goldthwaite.*

This photograph of Turkey Creek merchant Leverett Nellis and his wife Maud was taken during their early years in that community. *Courtesy Nell Nellis Goldthwaite.*

Turkey and not Turkey Creek because of a cumbersome postal regulation that prohibited duplication of a name even if the offices were in different states. The name of the post office caused some confusion among shippers but didn't bother folks familiar with the area.

Considering all the activity, surprisingly little building occurred in the town of Turkey Creek. The railroad men were housed in tents and hastily constructed shacks that moved with the construction crews as they worked their way to Crown King. A few new houses were built, but most of the local populace remained on the hillsides near the mines. Nellis' general merchandise and saloon buildings, along with his stable and barn, and the buildings of the B.M. Ry. were the only structures in town with the look of permanence. The railroad spur, instead of running parallel to the mainline as most spurs on the line did, veered south away from the right-of-way. Near the tail of the spur, the railroad constructed a 25 by 30 foot storehouse which was leased to merchants or mining companies. A tool house and several loading platforms were also railroad property.

It is interesting to note that the Bradshaw Mountain Railway had two spurs commonly referred to as Turkey Creek. The other "Turkey Creek Spur" was about a mile north of the community and near where the railway crossed a trestle high above the waters of Turkey Creek. A sign near the bridge identified the water below and contributed to the confusion as the spur stood just on the Crown King side of the trestle. Although seldom used, the five-car spur served a little livestock corral and stored empty railroad cars. The Turkey Creek shown on timetables was the spur in the community; the other spur was listed several pages into the old timetables under the heading "additional sidings and spurs not shown on regular timetable." The two spurs with the same name created much less confusion than might be expected as shipments going to Turkey Creek were shipped to the community promoted by Nellis.

Another men who had a lasting impact on the town arrived there in 1905. The personable newcomer was James P. Cleator. Cleator and the affable Nellis quickly developed a warm friendship and became partners in the Nellis General Store. They built a steady mercantile trade and promoted the little town. The freighting business did very well in the first months after the railroad reached the community.

The Nellis freighting enterprise delivered all types of materials and supplies from the Turkey Creek Spur to nearby mines. One of the supplies regularly shipped to the mines was dynamite. The dynamite of the day, unlike today's product, was highly unstable and very unpredictable. It could explode at the slightest provocation by temperature, humidity, or movement. Nellis, an excellent horseman, personally delivered much of the dynamite. Large shipments of the explosive were transferred in his buckboard; smaller orders were carried by pack animals led by Nellis. Stories abound of Nellis inviting friends to go horseback riding then horrifying them when he pulled sticks of dynamite out of his saddlebag. Nellis made dynamite deliveries without mishap for several years, but as word of his eccentricity spread, he did most of his horseback riding alone.

Although Turkey Creek did not grow as large as its merchants dreamed, it was a respectable little community. The population increased to forty by 1907, and the town was well known throughout the area. It did not enjoy the luxury of electricity but was proud of the town telephone in the general store. In the early days of the settlement, wells provided the community's water supply. The wells soon proved to be inadequate, and after the railroad arrived in town, a large cistern was built to store water. The railroad carried in drinking water from Mayer and made it available to the local residents. This awkward method of supplying water was replaced when the railroad constructed a pipeline from a well up the tracks near Middelton and pumped water to the cistern in Turkey Creek.

Turkey Creek had a small school prior to the turn of the century, but the school was not a permanent one. It was called into session only when the number of school-age children living in town required it. After several years of recess, the school was reopened in 1910. It had only two students and was too small to receive public funds. The school was privately financed and met in the back room of the town saloon. During most years, the local school children traveled to the grade school at Middelton.

The town did not have a law enforcement problem. The deputy sheriff in Mayer was relied upon to handle lawbreakers, but the community was generally a peaceful one. The town was very rough when the railroad construction crews were based there, but it quieted down after the crews moved on.

It appeared for a time that Turkey Creek might be the site of renewed railroad construction. There was talk of building a branch line to serve mines many miles south of Turkey Creek and even extending it to Phoenix. Nellis and Cleator promoted their town as the junction for the proposed railway. A group of Prescott businessmen, not affiliated with the Santa Fe,

The James Cleator General Store in Turkey Creek, circa 1914. *Courtesy Mynne Jarman.*

The railroad mainline passes in front of the James Cleator General Store at Turkey Creek and the spur cuts toward the Nellis house in that community. *Courtesy Nell Nellis Goldthwaite.*

incorporated the Prescott and Phoenix Shortline Railway Company in 1917 with the intent of building a branch line from the rail of the B.M. Ry. at Turkey Creek south to Phoenix. The poor showing of mines farther south and hard economic times ended talk about the new railroad. It is difficult to determine how the Santa Fe Railway felt about the proposed branch line, but Nellis and Cleator were certainly excited about the idea.

The business partnership between Nellis and Cleator was amicably dissolved circa 1909. Nellis remained active in the cattle ranching business which had been taking more and more of his time; Cleator became the sole owner of the store and saloon. The restaurant and freighting businesses had outlived their usefulness and were discontinued. The saloon, although still maintained by Cleator, was opened only upon request.

In 1913 Cleator constructed a new building for his general store in Turkey Creek. Only a few yards from the tracks, the false-front of the wooden structure proclaimed "James P. Cleator General Merchandise." The town phone and post office were moved into the new store, and Cleator became the postmaster. The new building was equipped with a generator and its own lighting system, as it was still several years before powerlines would be built to Turkey Creek.

Recreation in Turkey Creek was basically the

same as in other towns along the railroad line. The standard pastimes of dances, athletic contests, card playing, and holiday celebrations were much enjoyed, but some of the favorite pleasures were those of the palate. Nellis and Cleator had a recipe for homemade root beer that made mouths water. The concoction was very tasty, and they could not seem to make enough of it to keep everyone satisfied. Candy, popcorn, raisins, and locally picked walnuts were epicurean delights. An Edison phonograph, the pride of Maud Nellis, was listened to on special occasions and was used for dances, which were held every few weeks. Another gathering eagerly awaited in Turkey Creek was the yearly general election.

The townspeople displayed considerable interest in the general elections. The community was a polling place from the turn of the century. Initially called the Black Canyon Precinct, the name was changed to Turkey Creek Precinct in 1912. The store was the gathering place for the election, and votes were cast there. It may be remembered that residents of Cordes also voted in Turkey Creek, and the "get together" was always enthusiastic.

The town witnessed much activity during the early twenties when many local mines were reopened. The years 1920 to 1923 were very productive for the gold and silver mines near Turkey Creek, but the community's "golden years" were behind her. In 1919, Nellis retired and left the community. James Cleator made requests to the Post Office Department and to the railroad to have the name of the community officially changed to Cleator. The government granted his request in

May 1925, and the railroad did likewise in November 1926. The rail retreated from Crown King to Middelton in 1926 and left Turkey Creek in 1932.

After the railroad tracks were removed, Turkey Creek took on the appearance of a dying town. The population, which was forty-five in 1920, dwindled to only a few old-timers. James Cleator installed gas pumps in front of the store, and the W.P.A. built a stone schoolhouse in the community, but other improvements were few. Traffic on its way to summer cottages in Crown King and Horsethief Basin was all that kept the town alive. James Cleator put the community—lock, stock, and barrel—up for sale in 1949. At that time, it amounted to about twenty houses, the old store, gas pumps, and rudimentary waterworks. The population, including seasonal residents and ranchers from the vicinity, was sixty. Although the offer to sell the community received a great amount of publicity, the town was never sold and remains with the Cleator family.

Today, the Cleator General Store still stands just south of the roadbed. It has been closed for years but serves as a reminder of a bygone day. The railroad grade is under the auto roadbed, but the cut through the hillside into town is easily seen. Each spring when the road is graded by large caterpillar machinery, rusted railroad spikes and other corroded railroad hardware are unearthed and pushed off to either side of the dirt road. Only eighty years ago, the same roadbed was graded albeit with slightly different equipment and for a somewhat different mode of transportation.

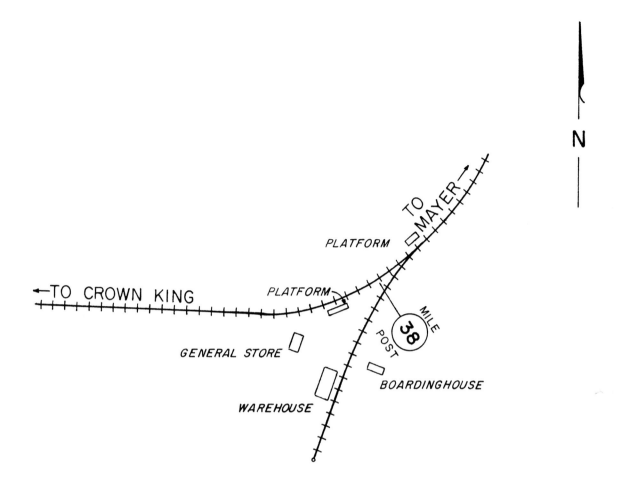

N

←TO CROWN KING

TO MAYER→

PLATFORM

PLATFORM

MILE 38 POST

GENERAL STORE

WAREHOUSE

BOARDINGHOUSE

TURKEY CREEK SPUR

SCALE: 1"= 200 FEET

MAP BY ROB KROHN

We are a welcome sight at the Middelton depot as we deliver fresh vegetables and bolts of cloth ordered from Prescott. The first and second switchbacks on the difficult ascent to Crown King are at Middelton; the engineer prepares his locomotive by taking on water and checking brass gauges. Behind the depot, a magnificent aerial tramway climbs the rugged mountain slope to the De Soto Mine high on the ridge.

MIDDELTON STATION

1903 - 1932

The route of the Bradshaw Mountain Railway, like the Prescott and Eastern, was determined by the location of several mines in which Frank Murphy and his associates held a financial interest. One mine upon which Murphy had a keen eye and which influenced the right-of-way of the Bradshaw Mountain Railway was the De Soto Mine. Located about three miles west of the community of Turkey Creek, the mine was high on McKinley Peak on the north side of Crazy Basin. Promoters called it "another Jerome" and wrote glowing accounts of the mine's worth. Murphy, and avid reader of assay results and production statistics, ordered a depot established at the foot of the mountain. The depot was christened Middelton, in honor of the owner of the mine.

Although the area was prospected as many as ten years earlier, the De Soto Mine was not discovered until September 1875. The mine was originally called the Buster Copper Mine but was also known at various times throughout the years as the Copper Cobre, Bradshaw Mountain Mine, and the name by which it is generally known—the De Soto. The early tunnels and operation of the mine centered on the north side of the ridge, although exploration on the southern slope was extensive. A short distance west of the De Soto were numerous prospector holes and several productive silver mines. A well-maintained road, over which ore shipments and supplies were dispatched and received, led from the silver camps to Prescott. A crude wagon road connected these camps to the nascent De Soto Mine.

A small mining camp west of the De Soto was originally the home of the men employed at the mine. This camp was utilized by the men of several mines and probably dated to the 1870s. In the early 1890s, a bunkhouse and blacksmith shop were constructed on the northern slope near the main tunnel and served as the base of operations. Although the camp moved to the mine site, transportation, communication, and social ties were still with the silver camps a couple of miles to the west.

The arrival of the railroad in Crazy Basin in 1903 caused a shift in emphasis at the De Soto from the northern to the southern slope of McKinley Peak. A new tunnel was blasted into the mountain from the south to intercept the rich ore deposits. A modern camp, including an assay office, office building, boardinghouse, cookhouse, blacksmith shop, warehouse, and corral, was built near the new tunnel and within sight of the railroad in the valley below. A road was carved to the railroad siding, and ore was delivered in wagons or on pack animals. Although the railroad was less than three-quarters of a mile below the mine, transportation to the railroad siding was still slow and costly. The mining company realized that a more efficient means of moving large amounts of ore to the siding was needed. After several weeks of consideration, the owners of the De Soto Mine built an aerial tramway to move their ore from the mine to the highway of steel.

The tramway, which was the best money could buy, was completed in April 1904. It was designed

This photograph shows the lower tramway terminal of the De Soto Mine in Middelton. The railway spur ran along the far side of the structure and a series of ore chutes directed the ore into railroad cars which waited beneath. *Courtesy Charles Nichols.*

by the Blechert Transportanlagen Company of Leipzig, Germany, and manufactured in this country by the Trenton Iron Works Company. The tramway was four thousand feet in length and had a daily capacity of two thousand tons. It operated entirely by gravity as the loaded buckets traveling down the mountain slope furnished the power to return the empty ones up the mountainside to the mine. During the first years of its operation, daredevil miners balanced precariously in the buckets and rode the tramway from the railroad siding to the mine. However, after a year or two of operation, even the most adventuresome declined rides, as mishaps occasionally caused battered ore buckets to fall to the rocky ravine two hundred feet below the tramway cables. It is not believed that any lives were lost riding on the tramway, but the tram was used on at least two occasions to lower caskets to the siding in Middelton. The caskets of a miner killed in a dynamite explosion and the wife of the mine foreman were lowered from McKinley Peak amid moist eyes, doffed hats, and noisy tramway cables.

While the tramway was being built on the mountain slope, Middelton was also the site of considerable construction activity. The railroad decided to make Middelton, which was halfway between Mayer and Crown King, the base camp for its maintenance workers. The site served as a temporary home for the construction crews as they worked their way toward Crown King and was later made the permanent camp of the men

responsible for maintaining railroad track and property on the Bradshaw Mountain Line. The railroad built a section workers' bunkhouse which was similar to a dormitory and also constructed a separate dwelling for the foreman and his family.

The railroad built and maintained numerous other buildings and structures in Middelton. The depot, which measured twelve by forty-eight feet, was connected by a wooden platform to a large adjacent warehouse. A house was built for the station agent assigned to the depot, and two other dwellings were built in the community for various purposes. A water tank, tool shed, and assorted platforms and storage structures were also railroad property in Middelton. During the days of track construction between the town and Crown King, a turntable was placed in Middelton to allow the engines to change directions for the trip back to Prescott. This turntable was removed after the rail was completed to Crown King.

In addition to the railroad, several other enterprises were represented in Middelton. The mining company owned the tramway terminal and a large powerhouse and maintained an office in the community. Wells Fargo and Western Union established offices in the depot and operated them in conjuction with the railroad. A post office was granted to the town on 8 May 1903, and George Middleton was named postmaster. In 1904, the population of the community was about seventy-five, while the population of the camp at the mine was near one hundred.

91

Railroad section workers pose in Middelton during 1917. *Courtesy Charles Nichols.*

The Middelton Depot was a busy place in 1904. *Courtesy Arizona Department of Library, Archives and Public Records.*

Frank Murphy took an early interest in the De Soto Mine. A first-rate businessman and promoter in his own right, Murphy had contacts and friends in all the right places. He was advised and kept abreast of mineral discoveries and noteworthy mining developments. Murphy invested in several mines, and considering the risk of that type of investment, he did rather well. He knew George Middleton, the developer of the De Soto Mine. The mine and Murphy's railroad presumably were discussed whenever the two met. Several factors indicate that Murphy was involved with the mine ownership either directly or indirectly as early as 1902. By 1905, he served on the Board of Directors of the Arizona Smelting Company, which owned the mine. Unfortunately, the De Soto was not as rich as many people, including Murphy and Middleton, had hoped.

Entrepreneurs attempted to duplicate the successful efforts of Charles Wingfield in Huron and Leverett Nellis in Turkey Creek by establishing saloons in Middelton. The town and De Soto Mine supported two saloons: one owned by Thomas Hogan, the other operated by Robert J. Schwanbeck. Schwanbeck was the first to open his doors in Middelton, doing so in 1903 shortly after the rail reached the community. Schwanbeck and his competitor never achieved the success they sought. Hogan stayed only briefly, while Schwanbeck eventually moved his establishment to Humboldt.

Schwanbeck and his wife attained a degree of notoriety for an event which occurred in 1907. Accidents were relatively common to mining and railroad towns. Often the experience of a miner or a railroader was measured by the number of scars he wore or by the number of fingers he was missing. The Schwanbeck mishap of September 1907 was a bit unusual even in a community accustomed to injuries. While pushing a baby stroller along the road in front of her house in Middelton, Mrs. Schwanbeck was bitten on the ankle by a large diamondback rattlesnake. Her husband was notified immediately and arrived home within fifteen minutes. He quickly opened the wound with his razor and in heroic fashion sucked the poison from it with his mouth. When the doctor from Crown King reached Middelton to

A look at the Middelton Depot a few days after it was completed in 1903. Note the turntable and the railroad trestle in the right-center of the photograph. *Sayre Collection.*

attend to the woman, he found her experiencing some pain but past the crisis stage. However, Mr. Schwanbeck was extremely ill as he had swallowed some of the poison while sucking it from the wound. After treatment, he recovered and was a good deal wiser for his experience. A lengthy article appeared in the Prescott newspaper casting the couple into celebrity status for a few days after it was printed. The hillsides near Middelton were infested with more than their share of rattlesnakes, for which the railroad workers and miners were constantly on the alert.

In 1904 when ore was first shipped over the Bradshaw Mountain Line from Middelton, the total production of the entire Peck Mining District was only $83. With the luxury of the railroad, this annual figure increased rapidly and reached $307,213 by 1906. Production and ore shipments received a major setback, however, in September 1904 when the Valverde smelter burned to the ground. Without a local smelter to process its ore and due to poor financial decisions, the company that operated the De Soto Mine was forced into bankruptcy.

The De Soto Mine lay dormant, and the miners left town. The merchants, in search of trade, were forced to leave Middelton. The post office was discontinued on 31 January 1908. The railroad depot was closed and boarded up, the agent's house was empty and neglected. Wells Fargo and Western Union deserted the community. Only a few section workers continued to be employed, as many of the mines in the Bradshaw Range were closed for financial reasons. With dwindling use, the rails received less maintenance. It was not long before a few railroad employees and a mine watchman were all that remained of the bustling little town. The population of Middelton was reduced to twenty-five by 1908.

With the railroad, large-scale operation of the mine disproved the proclamations that the De Soto was "another Jerome." The ore, which was spectacularly rich near the surface, diminished in quality with depth. The deposit was a large one, and great amounts of ore were mined, but the ore was only 3 percent copper. Although high by today's standards, the ore was considered low quality by the standards and technology of the day.

The town deteriorated until the mine was reactivated in 1914. During the mine's inactivity, the railroad leased two of its dwellings in Middelton to a rancher who raised cattle nearby. His dozen cattle outnumbered the human population of the community through the end of 1914. The loss of the powerhouse and one of the old saloon buildings to fire reduced the number of buildings in town, but the livestock and reptile population didn't seem to mind.

The enormous demand for copper generated by World War I reopened the De Soto Mine. The mine's ownership had undergone several reorganizations and was solvent by 1914. In August of that year, crews reconditioned the aerial tramway. Technological advances and improved mining methods made the mine very profitable, but the aspirations of ten years earlier were dashed forever. Miners returned to town, rail traffic increased, and more railroad employees were assigned to the community.

The town of Middelton was a busy community once again, albeit on a much smaller scale than a few years before. The railroad never assigned another station agent to the community, and the depot remained boarded up and closed. Wells Fargo and Western Union never returned, and the only merchant represented was James Cleator of Turkey Creek. He leased a portion of the railroad warehouse in Middelton and operated a little store there. His establishment featured a pool table, card

Passengers wait to board a coach of the Bradshaw Mountain Railway as it sits in front of the Middelton Depot. *Courtesy Mynne Jarman.*

tables, soft drinks (prohibition), and popular food and sundry items. The mining company office moved to the mine site, and inquiries, correspondence, and visitors were directed up the mountainside.

After a year of effort, the community was successful in having a post office re-established on 13 January 1916. In accordance with United States Postal Service regulations, which prohibited the recognition of a previously discontinued post office branch, another name had to be selected for the community's new post office. The name chosen was Ocotillo, and Pearl Orr was named the postmistress.

The residents of Middelton were employees of either the mining company or the railroad and their families. Middelton, during the years of World War I, housed approximately one hundred people. The miners were primarily Europeans, and the railroad section workers were mainly Mexicans. Supplies and fresh produce were generally ordered by telephone from Prescott. Although these items could be purchased from several trackside communities, prices were generally cheaper in Prescott. Storekeepers placed the goods on the southbound train and knew the return train would carry their payment. Blocks of ice for the family iceboxes were ordered from Mayer and delivered by the train. The railroad also transported the coal which it provided for its employees' use in their woodburning stoves. The railroad also, often unknowingly, provided the railroad ties that other residents used in their stoves.

Recreation in Middelton was simple yet satisfying. Dances were the favorite pastime of the men and were held often in Crown King and Turkey Creek. The bunkhouses witnessed innumerable card games, as that was also a popular form of entertainment. On the few occasions when snow stayed on the ground, snowball fights and throwing snowballs at the railroad water tank were cold but fun activities. Once a year, a traveling band of gypsies visited the community. The group's "dancing" bear was always a big hit with men and women and boys and girls of all ages. In late August, an annual picnic was held near Crown King. It included homemade ice cream, wild grapes, and walnuts. These annual events were delightful highlights for the residents of Middelton.

A dependable water supply was important to the railroad and the community. Most of the town's water came from the Blanco White Spring over a mile away. The railroad piped the water from the spring to its water tank in Middelton. Another small local well was also used to meet the town's

Youngsters enjoy a rare snowstorm in Middelton. The water tank and station agent's house are in the distance. *Courtesy Mynne Jarman.*

water needs. Yet another well and spring on the mountainside were not very reliable, and water for the boardinghouse at the mine was shipped up from Middelton via the tramway.

Despite the hardships, the townspeople were happy and stayed relatively healthy considering their isolation and occupations. If they did "take ill" country doctors in Mayer and Crown King still made house calls. Hospitals in Humboldt, Prescott, and McCabe (until 1907) treated the severely injured. Those that medical science could not help were buried in little cemeteries that still dot the countryside.

The majority of Middelton residents were single men; however, enough children were present by 1917 to necessitate the construction of a schoolhouse. The enrollment of the small, red, wooden structure never exceeded fourteen pupils, yet it housed all eight grades. Almost as important to the townsfolk was the wooden flagpole which stood beside the school. The American flag waved proudly from the pole for many years. Middelton's population never warranted such refinements as a church, fire department, or police force. The county sheriff was called whenever lawlessness required his presence.

The student body stands in front of the Middelton schoolhouse, circa 1917. *Courtesy Mynne Jarman.*

In this photograph of Middelton, several railroad buildings and much of the track are visible. *Courtesy Jack Orr.*

Although all the refinements of urban living were not present in Middelton, the residents of the community displayed civic pride. Voting was a privilege which was taken very seriously. Votes were cast in Middelton between 1904 and 1908; however, after the town was revived in 1915, the voters traveled to Turkey Creek to cast their ballots. Middelton was always well-represented at the polls.

Although strong in spirit, Middelton lacked many of the "modern" conveniences. The luxury of electricity was never enjoyed by the community. Some of the buildings on the hillside near the mine had electric lights, but most of them also relied upon kerosene lamps, as did the populace of Middelton. Telephone service was installed to the mine prior to 1901, but Middelton did not obtain this utility until 1915 when a party line running from Mayer to Crown King was installed. Roads led from Crown King and Turkey Creek to Middelton, but their poor condition prevented any but the sturdiest vehicles from reaching Middelton.

The railroad depot in Middelton was vacant during World War I, but the town witnessed increased railroad activity. The train crossed the trestle on the outskirts of town many times over the years. The sidings in Middelton could hold twenty-eight cars and were often filled to near capacity. Many of the ore cars were empty and destined for Crown King while others awaited copper ore from the De Soto. The rail witnessed decreasing activity, however, in the early twenties as Bradshaw Mountain mines one after another were worked out and abandoned.

Although the De Soto Mine produced a great deal of ore during World War I, it failed to live up to the expectations of its owners. In 1919, development work enlarged the limits of the ore bodies already known but did not result in any new discoveries. The days of great activity were numbered, as the company considered the mine to be completely developed and resigned itself to work it out gradually in accordance with market conditions. Work was discontinued at the property in 1922, and the mine was considered exhausted. The total yield of the De Soto Mine at that time was $3,250,000, which made it one of the largest producers in the Bradshaw Range, but no Jerome.

The days of hectic activity in Middelton had passed. Fewer than a dozen railroad employees made up the town's population as activity at the De Soto Mine ceased. On 15 June 1925, the Ocotillo Post Office in Middelton was discontinued. Middelton had a ghostly look in 1926 when a small company leased the De Soto and shipped a few carloads of low-grade ore. Various lessees continued operations at the mine until August 1930, when the lower two tramway towers and terminal were destroyed by fire. The mine was abandoned for the next quarter-century.

This view of Middelton is from beneath the aerial tramway on the mountain slope. *Courtesy Mynne Jarman.*

The Crown King Branch of the Bradshaw Mountain Railway fell into disuse and was abandoned. The tracks were pulled up and removed in sections beginning in 1926 with the Crown King to Middelton segment. The rail remained in Middelton until 1932, when it retreated even farther. The railroad razed the structures it owned along its right-of-way, which included its buildings in Middelton. The deserted schoolhouse and two abandoned residences were all that remained. These structures were burned, wrecked, or carried off by vandals, thieves, and natural elements prior to 1946. A similar fate befell the buildings at the mine site with the exception of a portion of the upper tramway terminal and several tramway towers, which still remain.

Today, Middelton and the surrounding area are deserted. The De Soto Mine, lying high on the rugged moutain slope from which more than $3,250,000 worth ore was carved, is silent. A stiff wind screams in its loneliness as it blows down the moutainside and across the abandoned landscape that was once filled with promise. The weathered and fallen timbers of the Bleichert aerial tramway, miles of frayed cables, and the weed overgrown railroad switchbacks are the last vestiges of the thriving Middelton community.

Silhouetted against the purple sky of sunrise, the weathered tramway towers still climb the slope toward the De Soto Mine. *Courtesy David Sayre.*

With Crazy Basin far in the distance, the gray, splintered tramway towers descend McKinley Peak as they have done for the past eighty years. *Sayre Collection.*

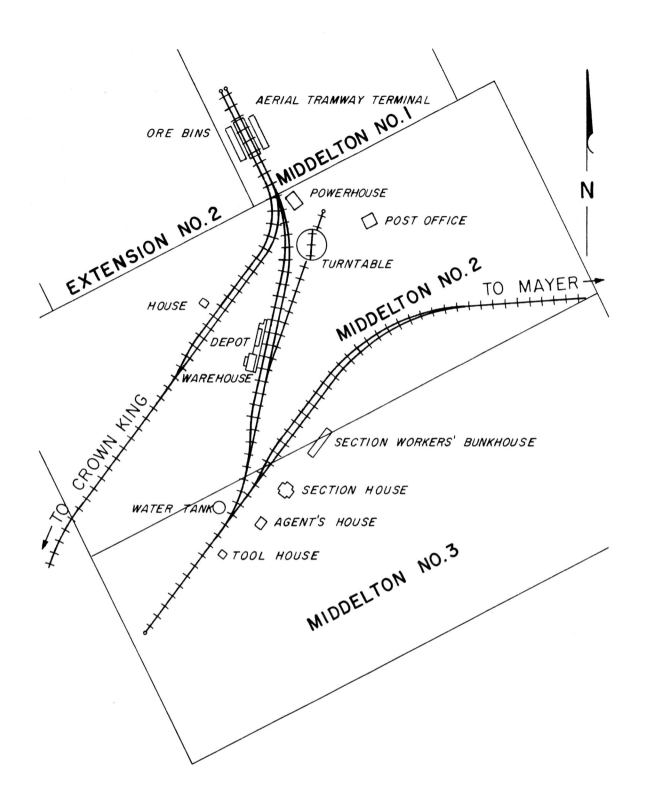

ORE BINS

AERIAL TRAMWAY TERMINAL

MIDDELTON NO. 1

EXTENSION NO. 2

POWERHOUSE

POST OFFICE

TURNTABLE

MIDDELTON NO. 2

TO MAYER →

HOUSE

DEPOT

WAREHOUSE

TO CROWN KING

SECTION WORKERS' BUNKHOUSE

SECTION HOUSE

WATER TANK

AGENT'S HOUSE

TOOL HOUSE

MIDDELTON NO. 3

N

MIDDELTON STATION

SCALE: 1"= 250 FEET

MAP BY ROB KROHN

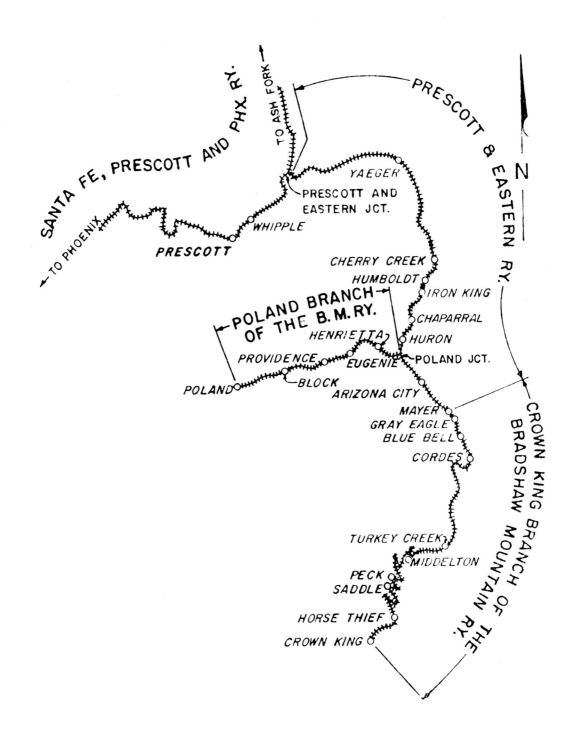

SANTA FE, PRESCOTT AND PHX. RY.

TO ASH FORK

PRESCOTT & EASTERN RY.

← TO PHOENIX

PRESCOTT

WHIPPLE

YAEGER

PRESCOTT AND
EASTERN JCT.

CHERRY CREEK

HUMBOLDT

IRON KING

POLAND BRANCH
OF THE B.M. RY.

CHAPARRAL

HENRIETTA

HURON

PROVIDENCE

EUGENIE

POLAND JCT.

POLAND

BLOCK

ARIZONA CITY

MAYER

GRAY EAGLE

BLUE BELL

CORDES

CROWN KING BRANCH
BRADSHAW MOUNTAIN OF THE
RY.

TURKEY CREEK

MIDDELTON

PECK

SADDLE

HORSE THIEF

CROWN KING

SCALE: 1" = 6 MILES

MAP BY ROB KROHN

We leave Middelton and begin the long climb to Crown King. The locomotive pants hard, and the astringent smell of steam and smoke drifts through the car. Just over two miles out of Middelton, we cross a massive steel and wood trestle known as the "Black Warrior." The structure, which is four hundred feet long and supports the rail nearly one hundred feet in the air, creaks as we stress its many timbers. Safely across, riprap supports the roadbed as we encounter the third pair of switchbacks and Peck Siding. The siding is empty, as the local mines have not been worked for several months.

PECK SIDING

1903 - 1926

The siding is about two miles southwest of, and is named for, the Peck Mine. The mine was discovered in 1875 and, along with the Tiger and Tip Top Mines, was one of the first rich silver discoveries in the mountains south of Prescott. The Peck Mine produced ore valued at $13,000 in its first few days of operation.

The news of the gleaming treasure traveled quickly, and soon hundreds of prospectors filled the hillsides, filed claims, and worked mines. Among the other mines that developed, the Black Warrior and Silver Prince were the most notable. These two silver-bearing mines, later known collectively as the Swastika Mine, produced over half-a-million dollars in ore by 1885. The Peck Mine, although embroiled in litigation for most of its early years, produced in excess of $1,200,000 in ore by the same year. The mines appeared so promising that a town, Alexandra, was established nearby in 1878. The town was short-lived but supported four to five hundred people, a brewery, hotels, saloons, and the usual assortment of businesses during its heyday.

The mines enjoyed extraordinary early success. Considering the rudimentary mining methods of the day and the fact that the ore was freighted at costs as high as $30 per ton to distant smelters, the production figures for the first years of mining operation were remarkable. The early years of the Peck Mine would have been more impressive had they not been marred by a lengthy and expensive court fight.

Lawsuits were no stranger to the mining industry in the Bradshaw Mountains or elsewhere. The legal entanglements often involved claim jumping, disputes over claim boundaries, and stock swindles. The lengthy litigation that tied up the Peck Mine was unusual in that it had some different twists.

One of the partners in the mine, William Cole, was enjoying immensely the financial and social rewards afforded the owner of a rich mine. In the spring of 1876, he left his cold, damp cabin at the mine for a few days of carousing and relaxation in Prescott. Known as a man who "tipped the bottle" for other than medicinal purposes, he embarked on a prolonged drinking spree in the tinseled saloons of "Whiskey Row." While "under the influence," Cole signed his ownership in the mine over to May Bean, the wife of one of his partners in the mine.

When Cole returned to sobriety, he brought suit to recover his ownership in the mine on the grounds that while intoxicated he was incapable of transacting business and therefore could not legally have transferred ownership. The case was interesting in that Cole's own attorneys portrayed him as an irresponsible, disgraceful drunkard, while the Beans' lawyers described him as hardworking, highly-respected, and the model citizen. The Prescott newspapers and townsfolk were divided on the character of Cole, and the issue was as hotly contested in the streets as it was in the courtroom.

The long-awaited decision was finally rendered and supported Cole. The judgment, which restored his ownership in the mine, was immediately appealed, again plunging the mine into the court docket. The other owners attempted to move some of the dirt-slinging from the courtroom to the mine tunnels. They incorporated the mine and placed the disputed 25 percent ownership and corresponding ore royalties in an escrow account. Suits, countersuits, and another attempt at incorporation followed.

The ore that was taken from the troubled mine was exceptionally rich. Armed guards accompanied the freight wagons that carried the ore to the Wells Fargo Office. Unfortunately, nearly all of the mine's profits went to line the pockets of the attorneys who handled the various lawsuits. The legal actions lingered for several more years. By the time the issues were finally resolved, Cole had died, and the other original owners, in order to pay legal expenses, sold out for a few thousands dollars each. The Peck Mine ultimately produced ore valued at more than $1,500,000.

The great years of production were already history, however, when Peck Siding was constructed in 1903. The siding, which held five cars, was only a flagstop on the journey to Crown King. A storehouse 10 by 32 feet was built at the siding and was used at different times by the railroad and operators of the local mines. The siding never witnessed the great activity that the railroad owners hoped its presence would stimulate.

Silver-tongued promoters proclaimed that the Peck and nearby mines would again be large, financially successful operations, but these fraud-ridden efforts produced more lawsuits than ore. Tailings were repeatedly reprocessed, and exploration continued, but the poor quality ore that remained only diminished further in value the deeper the miners dug. Legitimate operation of the Swastika Mine on a small scale through 1915 produced moderate amounts of ore, but mining in the area was more a memory than reality. Intermittent mining activity occurred after 1915, but unlike the first years the B.M. Ry. ran to the siding, ore shipments were few and small.

For the first several months that the railroad served Peck Siding, considerable quantities of ore were shipped. This ore had been mined and stockpiled over the previous few months and was not a true measure of production. The mines and the siding were major disappointments. Peck Siding and its namesake mine have been silent and deserted during most of the twentieth century.

Peck Canyon still shows the scars of last century's mining efforts. A few buildings stand at the Swastika Mine, but these are not the original structures and are much newer than commonly thought. The site of Alexandra is barely discernible and can be located only by the knowledgeable and persistent. At Peck Siding, portions of the switchback and railroad grade are visible and can be seen by hundreds of motorists on their way to summer cottages in Crown King and Horsethief Basin. When the rail was removed from Crown King to Middelton in 1926, Peck Siding's abandonment became official and final.

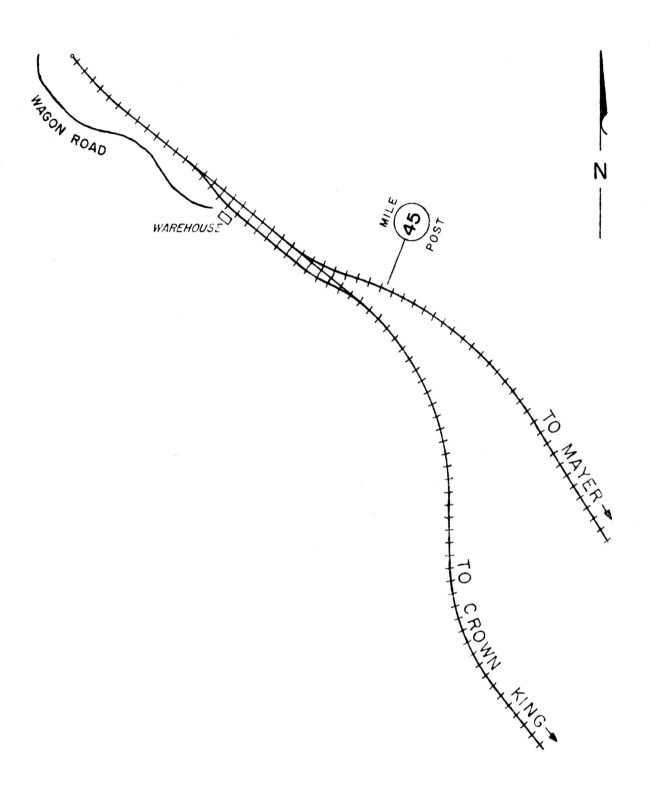

WAGON ROAD

WAREHOUSE

MILE 45 POST

N

TO MAYER

TO CROWN KING

PECK SIDING

SCALE: 1"= 200 FEET

MAP BY ROB KROHN

Black smoke pours from our smokestack as we crawl up the fourth pair of mountainside switchbacks. Travel is slow, difficult, and not for the faint of heart. This treacherous section of track, along with a section near Poland, is the most demanding and dangerous on the Bradshaw Mountain Line. Just over the summit, a collective sign of relief is heard from crew and equipment alike. We near Saddle Spur and cherish the sight of level terrain.

SADDLE SPUR

1903 - 1926

The track of the Bradshaw Mountain Railway was completed to the mountain summit between Middelton and Crown King in late October 1903. Less than three-fourths of a mile from Peck Siding as the crow flew, the difficult slope required almost three miles of rail to ascend the 2,000 vertical feet to the summit.

The slope was conquered by several pairs of ascending switchbacks which were constructed between Middelton and Saddle Spur. The trains slowly pulled onto the tail of the switchback and stopped beyond the switchstand that directed the cold, shiny rail. The switch was then thrown toward Crown King, and the engine cautiously backed the short distance to the next tail. Once safely on that tail, its switch was also repositioned. With a jerk, a moan, and a burst of steam, the train resumed its journey into the high country. The switchbacks were built in pairs, which allowed the engines to pull rather than push the cars except for the short distance in the middle of a particular pair of switchbacks. The section of rail between Middelton and the summit was an engineering feat, but an expensive one. Saddle Spur was scarcely two miles from Middelton, but seven miles of track, six hundred construction workers, six months of backbreaking labor, and hundreds of thousands of dollars were needed to complete that part of the line.

On 17 November 1903, a special excursion train was run to what was then the end of the line, Saddle Spur. Lines of people waited to board the train long before the 9:00 A.M. departure time.

The train was crowded when it left the Prescott depot, and several more passengers joined the excursion along the way. Miners, merchants, reporters, investors, and sightseers, an estimated three hundred people in all, packed the three coaches on the warm autumn day. Excitement filled the air, and good food filled the stomachs as lunch baskets stowed under the seats provided the "fixins" for a splendid picnic at Saddle Spur. The scenic view from the lofty summit and the extraordinary accomplishment of the construction crews were the talk of everyone on the train. The excursion was a resounding success, as it not only promoted the young railroad to local residents but also attracted widespread publicity not attainable at any price.

There was very little business tributary to Saddle Spur. Located to the left of the mainline for Crown King-bound trains, the spur was occasionally used as a safety outlet for northbound trains having equipment trouble. More often, the spur, its connection on the northern (Middelton) end, served as a storage facility for boxcars or extra ore cars. The spur only held two cars in addition to the engine and caboose. Although midway between mineral deposits of great wealth, there were no successful mines close to Saddle Spur. For that reason, regular service was not extended to the spur until the line was completed to Crown King in the spring of 1904.

This part of the line, although memorable to all who rode the rail, was a major disappointment to the owners of the Bradshaw Mountain Railway.

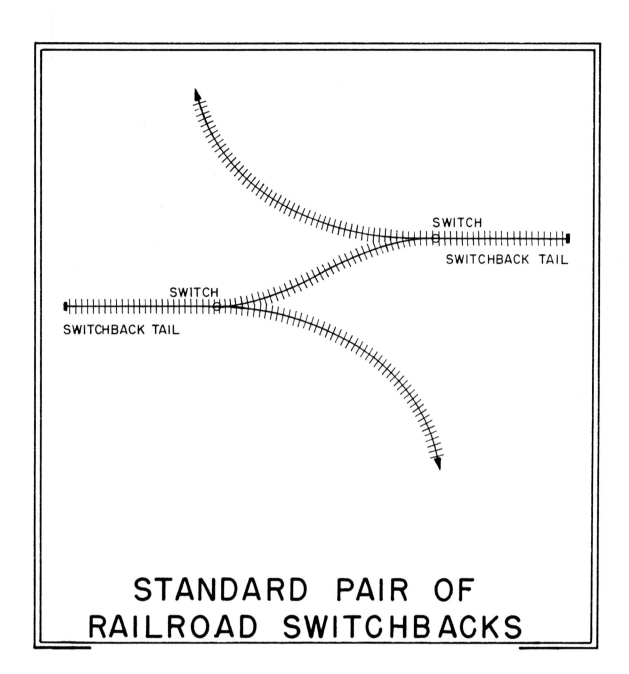

SWITCH

SWITCHBACK TAIL

SWITCH

SWITCHBACK TAIL

STANDARD PAIR OF
RAILROAD SWITCHBACKS

NO SCALE

MAP BY ROB KROHN

Due to the unstable nature of the landscape, rock and mudslides were common and costly problems. Retaining walls were constantly in need of repair, and safety was maintained only at a high price. During rains, even sand spread on the steep tracks to increase friction did not make the rail passable. The maintenance problems were expensive, but in themselves not insurmountable. However, the poor output of mines beyond Middelton did not merit the costly upkeep of this section of the line. The impressive engineering marvel soon turned to boondoggle and was abandoned and removed only twenty-three years after the great fanfare that accompanied its completion.

Today, the tails of the switchbacks to the summit can still be seen. The automobile roadbed makes use of the old railroad grade, but hairpin turns cut short the railroad switchbacks. The view remains magnificent. The last vestiges of Saddle Spur are the deteriorated railroad grade and nearby railroad tie fence posts.

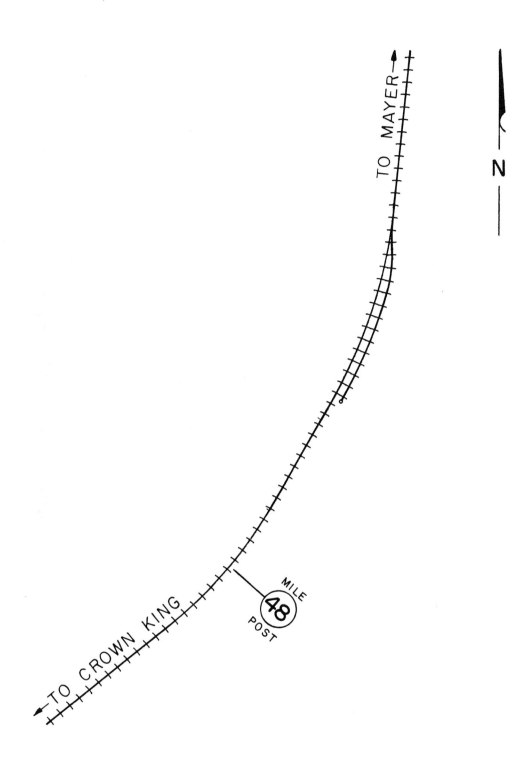

N

TO MAYER →

← TO CROWN KING

MILE
48
POST

SADDLE SPUR

SCALE: 1"= 200 FEET

MAP BY ROB KROHN

The last switchback and a tunnel hewn from solid rock stand between us and Horse Thief Spur on the Crown King Branch Line. As we steam toward the spur, the air is thin and cold; in the distance the pine trees are tall and thick. The rugged beauty of the countryside is an elixir for the soul. The locomotive, unaffected, senses she's in the homestretch and pulls hard for Crown King.

HORSE THIEF SPUR

1904 - 1926

Horse Thief Spur was near the head of, and named for, Horsethief Canyon. The spur, which was two miles from the town of Crown King and only one mile from the Crown King railroad yard limit, was completed in May 1904 during the big drive to reach Crown King. Capable of holding three cars, the spur had its connection on the south (Crown King) end of the mainline and was 360 feet long.

Horse Thief Spur served mining operations in Horsethief Canyon and elsewhere in the Pine Grove Mining District. Several small mines were discovered very early in Horsethief Canyon but

produced relatively little ore. The only mine that enjoyed much production was the Algonkian. The Algonkian Mine was moderately wealthy and produced ore rich in lead, silver, and copper.

In 1917, additional ore deposits were discovered in Horsethief Canyon, and the owners of the Algonkian Mine immediately pushed for a railroad spur to be built to their mine. Although the mining company funded a land survey for an extended spur to the mine, production simply did not justify additional railroad construction. To the chagrin of the mining company, the extended spur idea never came to more than that. The mining company was

This photograph shows construction crews laying rail a few miles from Crown King.
Courtesy Sharlot Hall Museum.

culpable as it maintained its office in Crown King, and while ore and equipment shipments made use of Horse Thief Spur, much of the company business was conducted through Crown King. There were no buildings, railroad or otherwise, at the spur.

Today, Horsethief Canyon is still a very picturesque area. the short railroad spur was abandoned and removed along with the mainline from Middelton to Crown King in 1926. Within the canyon, a few signs of mining activity are visible, but at the spur itself the railroad grade is all that remains.

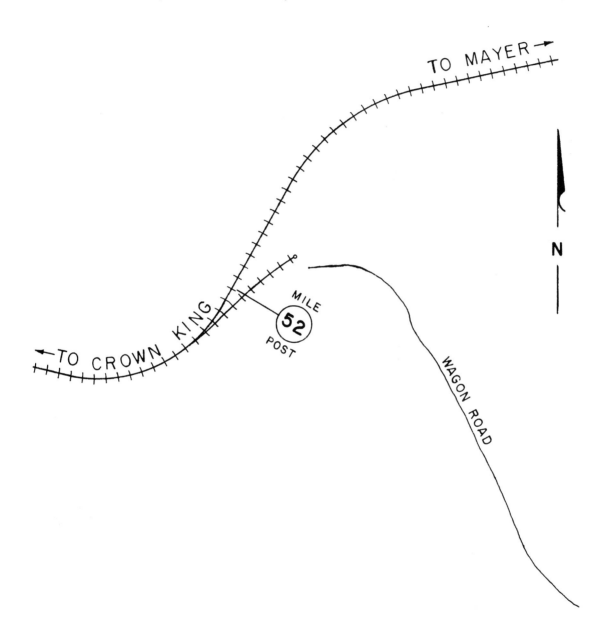

HORSE THIEF SPUR

SCALE: 1" = 250 FEET

MAP BY ROB KROHN

CROWN KING STATION

1904 - 1926

The rail of the Bradshaw Mountain Railway reached Crown King in the late spring of 1904 and stimulated renewed interest in the mountainside community and local mines. The railroad laid its track and constructed its numerous buildings near Poland Creek about a mile south of the Crowned King Mine and one-half mile from the camp that served the mine. Business establishments and private dwellings quickly appeared near the railroad buildings, and most activity shifted to the new area of settlement. It did not take long before the road from the mine to the railroad spur was lined with buildings of all types. Many mines, including the Wildflower, Del Pasco, and Philadelphia, enjoyed increased production attributable to the arrival of the railroad in Crown King. The excellent production histories of these mines no doubt influenced the decision to build the railroad line to Crown King, but it was the rich Crowned King Mine that brought publicity, investors, and ultimately the railroad to the mountain village.

The Crowned King Mine was a discovery which dated to the early 1870s. Located and quickly abandoned as both the Red Rock and the Buckeye Mines, the property came to the attention of N.C. Sheckels in 1888. Sheckels claimed the property and renamed it the Crowned King. Along with two partners, Sheckels formed the Crowned King Mining Company and began actively working the mine in January 1890. A small community that consisted of two boardinghouses, an assay office, and a store developed a short distance down the

slope from the mine. The mine produced good quality ores in 1891, and much needed improvements were started on the road to Prescott.

The region was extremely rugged, and the roads to the Crowned King Mine were narrow, rocky, and dangerous. The mining company packed its rich ore and concentrates forty miles over the treacherous, winding road to Prescott. The freight rates were prohibitively high, reaching $21.50 to $30 per ton. The roads were also used by freight teams that hauled logs to the mine for use as support timbers in the tunnels and as fuel. The Crowned King Mine was included on several stage routes, but the roads were so terrifying that many visitors never ventured over the rugged terrain a second time.

Despite the difficulties encountered in transporting ore, the Crowned King and nearby mines came of age during the decade of the 90s. The Crowned King was tied up in litigation from 1892 to 1898 but still produced great amounts of ore. Even during its legal battle, the mine was one of the most active in the Bradshaws. Production went so well that the company ran electricity to many of its buildings in 1896 and even added a telephone. The underground tunnels of the mine were also wired for electricity and made the mine one of the most modern and best illuminated of its time. In 1899, an extremely rich deposit of ore was unearthed in the Crowned King Mine that caused excitement among stockholders and investors. Samples of the gold ore were displayed in Prescott, and the town was intoxicated with reports of immense wealth. This strike at the Crowned King Mine and ownership of the nearby Wildflower Mine by Frank Murphy probably were determining factors in the decision to build the railroad line to Crown King. People began dropping the "ed" off Crowned King as early as the 1880s, but both spellings persisted for several years.

The severe high country winter of 1903 - 1904 was unrelenting on the railroad crews working toward Crown King. The crews dwindled in size, and even the hardiest workers were discouraged as they fought desperately to stay warm in the bitter cold. Construction was halted as snow, blown by violent icy winds, swirled through the mountains and drifts reached record heights. Gradually, the white blanket thinned and receded from the slopes. Work on the grade resumed but was hampered by wet and muddy conditions. The countryside was immersed in the green and warmth of spring before much progress was actually made.

After considerable delays, frustration, and expense, the railroad finally rolled into Crown King, elevation 6,000 feet, on 12 May 1904. Construction crews completed numerous railroad buildings in the community. One of the first buildings finished was the depot, which measured 20 by 94 feet. The baggage and freight portion of the building alone was larger than most other depots on the line. A house was constructed nearby for the station agent assigned to the community. Across the mainline from the depot, a twenty-four foot diameter water tank was built to serve the thirsty steam locomotives. A large tool house and a gasoline storage facility were built on the outskirts of town away from most of the other structures.

Numerous loading platforms, holding bins, and warehouses were scattered about town. Several different mining companies leased or utilized railroad property in Crown King. Separate spurs were laid in Crown King to serve three different mining operations. One spur served the Crown King Mine; the other two spurs served the Tiger Mine and the Philadelphia Group of mines. A siding capable of holding thirty cars was also built within the railroad yard in Crown King. The railroad track in Crown King was constructed in a wye configuration.

Like Middelton, Crown King was the home base for a crew of section workers. Bunkhouses for them, as well as a dwelling for the crew foreman, were also built in town and were not far from the water tank. The responsibilities of the section crew ranged from creosoting ties and replacing rail to painting buildings and repairing bridges. The

thirteen mile stretch between Middelton and Crown King constantly needed maintenance of one form or another, and the crews from the two communities did their best to keep the track and structures in safe condition.

The town of Crown King kept pace with the rapid growth of mining in the area. As mentioned earlier, the town enjoyed the luxuries of phone service and electricity as early as 1896. Wells Fargo and Western Union established offices in the community in 1904. N.E. Anderson served as agent for both companies as well as for the railroad from his window in the Crown King depot. A post office was granted to the hamlet on 29 June 1888 under the name Crown King. The post office did an exceptional business for a camp of Crown King's size as the miners there were reportedly among the most literate in the Bradshaws.

Much of the mail and most of the supplies for Crown King came from Phoenix before 1904. Crown King was in the southern portion of the Bradshaw Mountains and did not develop strong ties to Prescott as many of the camps farther north did. Although more distant, Phoenix offered better roads, lower prices, and more selection in most product lines. After the railroad reached Crown King, the obvious ties were with Prescott, and trade was with that community via the railroad.

The population of Crown King fluctuated greatly depending on local mining activity. Prior to the turn of the century, the population fluctuated from fifty to six hundred. The figures leveled out at about two hundred by 1907. At that time, the town supported four saloons, three freighting companies, two general stores, two restaurants, a laundry, seven mining company offices, the hospital of Dr. J.K. McDonald, and the Crown King Cemetery.

A school was established in Crown King shortly after the arrival of the railroad. Records show the community maintained a schoolhouse in 1904 but also show that a school teacher was not hired until 1908. Nearby Oro Belle had a school much earlier, and children from Crown King undoubtedly attended this school until the local school opened. With a few exceptions, the Crown King school bell rang every year from 1908 until well after the railroad left the community.

Education and literacy were very important to the residents of Crown King, as was the right to vote. The primary elections were almost as popular as the general elections in the little town. The Republicans, although outnumbered almost two to one, were a noisy group and gathered at the schoolhouse to choose their candidates. The Democrats gathered at the Crown King Mining Company office to select their nominees for the

The Crown King Depot and water tank are in the middle left of this photograph. Other notable buildings in town include: the general store, which is partially hidden by the depot, the Tiger Gold Company warehouse (E), the section house (F), railway agent's house (G), bunkhouse (H), and the section workers' bunkhouse (I). Notice the engine taking on water in front of the depot has a boxcar and a combination-coach in tow. *Courtesy Arizona Historical Foundation, Hayden Library, Arizona State University.*

November ballot. In 1904, sixty-one votes were cast in the general election; it is interesting to note that nine of those votes endorsed the Socialist Party. The same voting trend continued for several years. In 1912, the Democratic Party again carried the local vote twenty-four to twelve, with three votes for the Progressive Party and ten for the Socialists.

Aside from the thirst for political involvement, the community faced a thirst of another type. In the early days of the settlement, the water supply for the camp came from wells and the creek. These sources were not dependable during the dry months and were sometimes tainted by mining operations. To alleviate the problem, the railroad constructed a pipeline from Blanco White Spring near Middelton and piped the water twelve miles to its storage structures in Crown King. The town water supply was never in doubt after the pipeline was completed.

This turn-of-the-century photograph shows the work crew of the Gladiator Mine near Crown King. Notice that several of the men have in hand their candleholders which provided the only source of underground illumination. *Courtesy Arizona Department of Library, Archives and Public Records.*

Despite the hardships of living in a mountaintop community that was bitterly cold in the winter, the residents managed to keep a sense of humor. Jokes and stories were popular forms of entertainment, as were reading and letter writing. Drinking at the local saloons and card playing also received attention from many of the men. By 1897 the sport of tennis bounced into the community. An area was graded in front of the boardinghouse in Crown King, and a net was erected. The sport enjoyed considerable popularity for several weeks until the novelty wore off. The court was seldom used after the first few months. Bicycling and ping-pong were popular at the camp after the turn of the century, but the former was severely limited by the terrain—the only level spot in town was the tennis court. Dances and celebrations were always anticipated with much excitement. Local groups, such as the miner's union, promoted social activities and holiday celebrations.

The Western Federation of Miners (W.F.M.) was a strong labor union in the Bradshaws for a brief time after 1903. The union pushed for safer working conditions for the miners, shorter work days, and more pay. The Crown King miners belonged to the "Tiger Union" local of the W.F.M. The local, although not nearly as strong as chapters in McCabe and Jerome, was still active in community affairs. Labor Day and Fourth of July celebrations were sponsored by the union and were usually held in McCabe or Humboldt. People traveled from miles away to attend the festivities. The Western Federation of Miners later merged with the Industrial Workers of the World and created labor unrest in Jerome, Bisbee, and elsewhere during World War I. By the time labor strife hit the other areas, the miners in the Crown King area were lucky to be working at all, and labor union activities were all but forgotten.

Dr. McDonald and the Crown King Cemetery received much more business than anyone liked. The mines around Crown King were very dangerous, as were all mines of the time. Safety precautions in the mining industry were few, and cave-ins, explosions, and falling rock claimed a heavy toll in human suffering. Mining accidents were the primary source of serious injury and death, but were joined by stagecoach mishaps,

Frank Murphy and associates made several trips to Crown King and inspected mining properties there. In this photograph, Murphy is accompanied by W.A. Drake, general manager of the S.F., P. & P. and by W.F. Staunton, who oversaw Murphy's mining operations. To the left is the Crown King Depot; to the right is Murphy's personal railroad car; and in the distance is rich mining country. *Courtesy Arizona Historical Foundation, Hayden Library, Arizona State University.*

disease, suicide, and murder in reducing the Crown King population.

At least seventeen men were killed in arguments in Crown King in the 1890s. Most of the arguments were over women. At least two additional deaths were suicides by men who searched in vane for their "fortune in gold" and came up empty-handed. Crown King folklore has it that the infamous Poncho Villa worked briefly in town as a woodcutter during his younger years and got his "start" there. Whether or not Poncho Villa actually spent his "formative years" in Crown King is in some doubt, but the town was indeed a rough place before the turn of the century.

Crown King did not have a deputy sheriff during its early lawless days. The closest constable at that time was in the county seat, Prescott. Early lawlessness in the camp was not confined to drifters or malcontents but was prevalent even among community leaders. In March 1894, two of the community's most notable residents, O.F. Place and George P. Harrington, were embroiled in a court battle over the ownership of the Crowned King Mine. They met in Taylorsville, Illinois, at a meeting of the Board of Directors of their mining company in an attempt to work out their differences. Place made some comments to Harrington and his attorney with which the latter took issue. Place, annoyed and frustrated by the man's retort, reached into his valise for his gun. Bystanders tried to intervene, but Place removed his pistol and attempted to shoot Harrington's attorney. Quick-acting onlookers wrested the weapon from Place, but not before he pulled the trigger. Fortunately, the hammer fell on the outstretched hand of a gentleman trying to subdue Place, and the pistol did not discharge.

In an attempt to maintain law and order, the county stationed several constables in the Bradshaw Mountains by 1907. Ironically, by the time that the lawmen were assigned to the communities of Oro Belle, McCabe, Mayer, Poland, and Humboldt, the real need for the constables had passed. By the turn of the century, with few exceptions, large corporations dominated the mining industry. They had stockholders and directors to answer to, and lawlessness by any part of the work force or townspeople was simply not tolerated. The Crown King Mill storeroom was occasionally used to cool off and hold lawbreakers until a deputy sheriff was summoned. However, there was not much trouble after the turn of the century.

Ore production in the Pine Grove and the Tiger Mining Districts, which were served by the Bradshaw Mountain Railway terminus in Crown King, reported huge increases in production after the arrival of the railroad. In 1903, the total value of the ore produced in the districts was just over $41,000. In 1904, during the first year of railroad service, it doubled and in 1905 reached an all time high of more than $339,000. Although dropping off somewhat to $108,000 in 1907, the quantity of ore shipped "showed well" for both the mines and the railroad.

Unfortunately, 1907 was one of the last years of high ore production. The next four years were very disappointing in terms of mineral mined and new discoveries. Production bounced back in 1912 and 1913 to once again hit six figures, but the future of mining in the area was very much in doubt. Many of the mines were important producers in the last decade of the nineteenth century, but they were shallow gold ores and disappeared or became complex ore at depth. Closed or abandoned mines outnumbered active ones in 1914.

Frank Murphy purchased several mines in the Crown King area in 1909. He owned the Wildflower from many years earlier and added to that the property of the Crown King Mine, Tough Nut, and the Tiger. His efforts to locate additional ore bodies and develop the mines with an eye to the future proved fruitless. The most productive years around Crown King were prior to 1908. Tailings were reprocessed and produced some new ore, but this was limited in quantity.

Very few mines operated near Crown King by 1919. A brief resurgence occurred between 1916 and 1918 due to the wartime demand for copper, but the market collapsed as the war ended. Little ore remained in the mines, and to make matters worse, the railroad imposed a 25 percent rate increase on ore shipments in 1920. The mining and railroad industries were both in desperate shape.

Rail service to Crown King was cut back after World War I ended. The six day per week schedule maintained during the war was shortened to Tuesday, Thursday, and Saturday. This was curtailed even further in November 1920 when scheduled trains arrived only twice a week. Ore production was embarrassingly small in 1920, and the amount of ore shipped did not even come close to paying for the maintenance of the rail that served Crown King. The next two years were just

as bad, and the railroad began to sell and long-term lease some of its property in Crown King. It was only a matter of time before the rail was forced to retreat from the ailing mining districts near the mountaintop community.

The town of Crown King continued to endure in 1920, the population remained at about two hundred. Offices of four mining companies were maintained in town, the hotel and general store still served the local population, and the post office continued to post and deliver mail. The town had a constable and a justice-of-the-peace, a notary and a music teacher, and a billard hall and a school, but the economic base of the community was shattered.

The railroad retreated from Crown King to Middelton in 1926. A final excursion train ran to the town in November of that year allowing people from throughout the region to visit the town by rail one last time. The carnival atmosphere was enjoyed by all, but misty eyes prevailed as the locomotive pulled from the depot and headed down the mountain on its last official run. The railroad sold several of its town lots and some of the buildings before leaving Crown King. Other structures were razed to lower taxes and decrease liability from accidents. The rail was removed and used elsewhere in the Santa Fe System but only for sidetracks, as it was smaller than the size then used for mainline. Some of the rail was also salvaged for its scrap value. The ties were sold to, given to, and stolen by townspeople for use in building projects or as firewood.

Surprisingly, after the collapse of the mining industry in the region and the abandonment of the railroad, Crown King managed to survive. Fortunately for the local economy, residents from Phoenix discovered the area as a wonderful place to escape the brutal heat of summer. The population increased to 275 by 1941 as the cool summer breezes and sweet smell of pine attracted new residents to the area. Many of the old mining claims were subdivided and sold as cabin lots. Retirement and summer cottages mingled with old buildings in Crown King.

Today, the old general store, saloon, schoolhouse, and an occasional altered railroad building still stand in Crown King. Newer structures abound, and construction continues on the nearby slopes. The road travels the Bradshaw Mountain Railway roadbed into town, and many of the grades and the wye are still visible. In the hills around Crown King, some mining still takes place on a small scale, but the community relies upon tourists and seasonal residents for its survival.

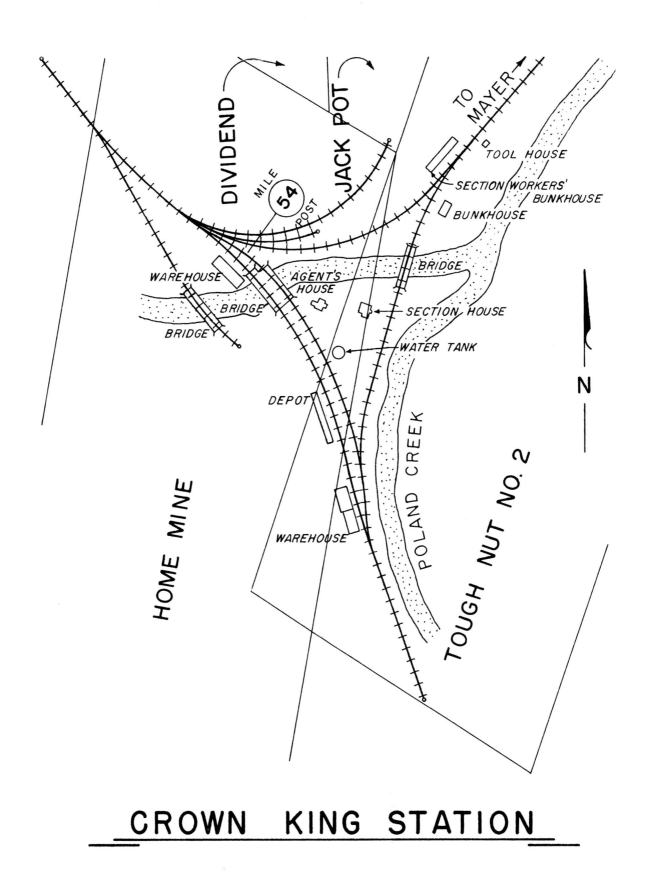

DIVIDEND

JACK POT

TO MAYER→

TOOL HOUSE

SECTION WORKERS' BUNKHOUSE

BUNKHOUSE

MILE POST (54)

WAREHOUSE

AGENT'S HOUSE

BRIDGE

BRIDGE

BRIDGE

SECTION HOUSE

WATER TANK

DEPOT

HOME MINE

WAREHOUSE

POLAND CREEK

TOUGH NUT NO. 2

N

CROWN KING STATION

SCALE: 1"= 200 FEET

MAP BY ROB KROHN

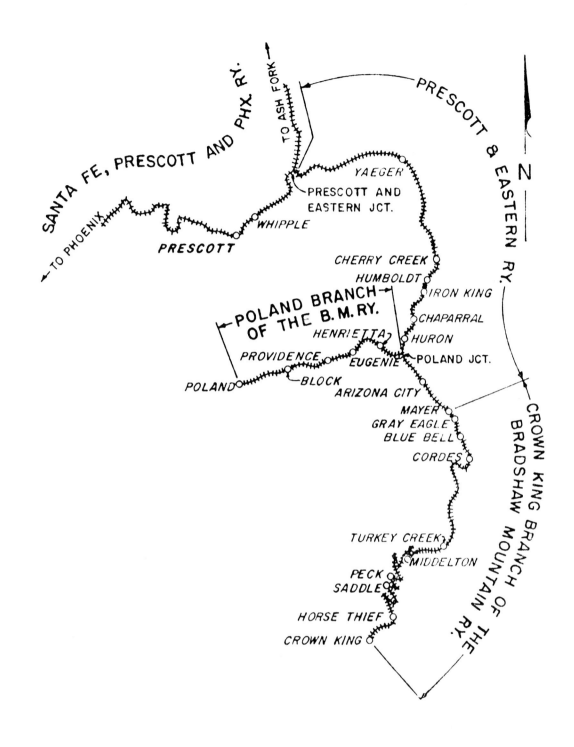

SANTA FE, PRESCOTT AND PHX. RY.

TO ASH FORK

PRESCOTT & EASTERN RY.

N

YAEGER

PRESCOTT AND
EASTERN JCT.

TO PHOENIX

WHIPPLE

PRESCOTT

CHERRY CREEK

HUMBOLDT

IRON KING

POLAND BRANCH→
OF THE B. M. RY.

CHAPARRAL

HENRIETTA

HURON

PROVIDENCE

EUGENIE

POLAND JCT.

POLAND

BLOCK

ARIZONA CITY

MAYER

GRAY EAGLE

BLUE BELL

CORDES

CROWN KING BRANCH
BRADSHAW MOUNTAIN OF THE RY.

TURKEY CREEK

MIDDELTON

PECK

SADDLE

HORSE THIEF

CROWN KING

SCALE: 1"= 6 MILES

MAP BY ROB KROHN

The journey down the mountain from Crown King to the foothills is just as exciting as the ascent. Wildlife abounds; deer, rabbit, and quail are common to the hillsides. The locomotive breathes much easier going down the switchbacks than it did going uphill, but the passengers and crew don't. The view is truly spectacular and makes the cliff-hanging ordeal worthwhile. Several ore cars loaded with copper ore and destined for the smelter at Humboldt are picked up at Middelton. The long string of ore cars rattles and shakes as it follows us down the rail into Big Bug country. We leave the ore cars on the siding at Poland Junction and head into the slowly sinking sun.

Heading west from Poland Junction, Big Bug Creek churns in the rocky ravine to our left. Mine tunnels and yellowish waste dumps dot the brush-covered slopes to our right. The Henrietta Spur serves many of these mines, including the old Big Bug or Henrietta Mine. We approach the spur in mid-afternoon and hear the sounds of mining machinery echoing from high on the mountain slope.

HENRIETTA SPUR

1902 - 1939

The Henrietta, or Big Bug Mine as it was called during its early years, was one of the original mineral discoveries in the Bradshaw Mountains. Pockets of gold and large insects were discovered in the creek in 1863. The creek was named for the huge bugs found in it, and the rich mine on the slope to the north of the creek also received the name Big Bug. The mine, which produced gold ore mixed with some silver and copper, was a steady producer from the time of its discovery. A ten-stamp mill was built on the creek in 1866 to process the mine's ore. Production increased as improved equipment was obtained, and the Big Bug was considered a major producer by 1884. Renamed the Henrietta, operation of the mine remained profitable, although intermittent, at the turn of the century.

Numerous mines overlooking Big Bug Creek were well-developed and had excellent production records by 1898. The promoters of the Bradshaw Mountain Railway sought both to stimulate mining activity in the area and to tap the wealth of the rich, established mines. Farther up Big Big Creek, the mines near Providence and Poland

helped entice the railroad into the higher elevations, but the Henrietta and its history of steady production also influenced the decision to build the branch railroad to Poland.

A small camp had developed along the creek below the mine by 1879. The camp consisted of several cabins and a row of stone houses that sporadically dotted the banks of the creek and stretched nearly three miles to where Providence later developed. A stage station, saw mill, two stores, and a little hotel served the camp. A post office, under the name Big Bug, was granted to the camp on 31 March 1879 and was established in the cabin of Theodore W. Boggs.

Boggs, the camp's postmaster and most notable resident, was a pioneer of the Big Bug area. He arrived there in 1863 and, along with his prospecting partners Davis R. Poland and John M. Roberts, made several rich discoveries. The Henrietta and De Soto, along with numerous other mines near Poland and elsewhere, were discovered by the prospecting trio. Boggs was quite a story in and of himself. His mother was the granddaughter of Daniel Boone, and his father was at one time the

118

Governor of Missouri. At the age of ten, Theodore W. Boggs was a member of the tragic Donner Party. Nearly half of the party perished on the way to California in the snow-laden Sierra Mountains. The survivors exhausted their food supply and resorted to cannibalism, thereby managing to hold on until rescued.

No stranger to adversity, Boggs endured several skirmishes with the Indians who, at the time of his arrival, controlled the Big Bug country. He was truly a "survivor" and lived a long life in the Bradshaw Mountains. He lived long enough to see the railroad serve the area that forty years earlier was beyond the outskirts of civilzation in the middle of Apache territory.

The "Big Bug Railroad," as many of the locals referred to the Poland Line of the Bradshaw Mountain Railway, reached the area below the Henrietta Mine early in 1902. The colorful history of Boggs was interesting, even at the turn of the century, but the railroad financiers had hopes that more "color" would be discovered in the local mines. Production figures at the Henrietta and nearby mines were very encouraging the first few years they were served by the railroad. The railroad constructed a spur to serve the mines in 1902 and appropriately named it for the Henrietta Mine. The spur had its connection on the south (Poland) end and was 339 feet long. The railroad also built a large loading platform at the spur, and the mining company built a twenty-five- by fifty-foot holding bin to store its ore. The spur held six cars and, during busy years, was usually filled to capacity.

The camp below the mine failed to develop and was in a deteriorated condition when the railroad was constructed. The mainline and the Henrietta Spur were several hundred yards above where the old camp buildings stood along the creek. The camp was largely neglected as the focus of activity shifted to Providence and farther up Big Bug Creek to Poland. Most of the buildings were vacant and abandoned by the turn of the century, but the post office remained in operation until 1910.

The Henrietta Mine eventually produced $1,250,000 worth of ore. The bulk of that production was prior to 1910 when the mine first closed. The mine was reopened from 1914 to 1919 when the mill on the property shipped considerable quantities of ore over the railroad to the Humboldt smelter. After 1919, shipments were few and small. Some ore shipments were made in 1923, 1926, and the mid-thirties, but large-scale activity at the mine ceased in 1919.

Another spur was constructed at Henrietta in 1917. The original spur remained and received some use, but the new spur, which was 1,800 feet long, received most of the activity. This new spur was financed and owned by the Big Ledge Copper Company and was not railroad property. The spur had its connection on the Poland end, as did the original spur, and cut from the mainline about a quarter-mile west of the old spur. The lengthy spur ran parallel to its predecessor, was also on the north side of the mainline, and was about five hundred feet closer to the mountain slope. The mining company removed this spur when it shut down operations in 1919.

Another camp developed at the mine during its World War I years. Bunk and boardinghouses were home for approximately one hundred men. A small local school was established but was only in session from 1917 through 1919. Mail was received at the Huron Post Office, and the makeshift camp at the Henrietta did not have the look of permanence. The new camp disappeared shortly after the mine closed in 1919.

The rail from Poland to the Henrietta Spur was removed seven years earlier, but the section of rail from the Henrietta Spur to Poland Junction remained intact until 10 April 1939. After that time, only a stem of the old wye to Poland remained.

Today, yellowish waste spills down the hillside beneath the Henrietta Mine, and the mountain is pockmarked with unsightly scars of yesteryear. Excavation continues occasionally, while modern mining equipment and "no trespassing" signs stand at the base of the 5,700 foot slope. Water trickles in Big Bug Creek during the "wet season," but most of the creek is on private property, which is also posted "no trespassing." Recent grading and the current road make the old railroad grade difficult to locate, but some of it can still be seen below the Henrietta Mine.

N

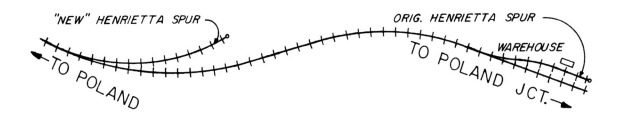

"NEW" HENRIETTA SPUR

ORIG. HENRIETTA SPUR

WAREHOUSE

TO POLAND

TO POLAND JCT.

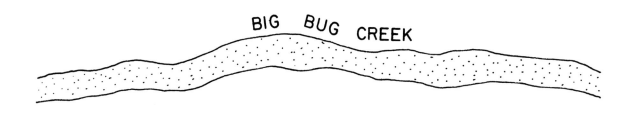

BIG BUG CREEK

ORIGINAL AND "NEW"
HENRIETTA SPURS

SCALE 1"= 250 FEET

MAP BY ROB KROHN

On our way to the next spur, which is called Eugenie, we encounter a group of railroad section workers repairing a drainage culvert. The foreman, tanned and crusty, complains about the weather and discusses track conditions with our engineer. On the spur itself, a solitary ore car with the Santa Fe logo sits empty.

EUGENIE SPUR

1902 - 1932

A mile-and-a-half west of Henrietta Spur was a spur called Eugenie. The spur was named for Eugenie Gulch, which the right-of-way crossed just southwest of the spur. Although the Eugenie Mining Claim was near the spur, the mine that was commonly known as the Eugenie was about a mile west of the spur in Eugenie Gulch.

Several mining claims were worked in Eugenie Gulch, but none developed into large producers. Small deposits of gold and silver were discovered there before the turn of the century, and the financial backers of the Bradshaw Mountain Railway hoped great mines would soon fill the gulch. Discoveries proved to be few, disappointing mining and railroad men alike, but dreams of that one big strike kept hopes alive for several years.

Optimism, if not valuable mineral, filled Eugenie Gulch in 1902 when the railroad constructed a spur to serve the area. The spur was 530 feet long, held eight cars, and like most spurs on the Poland Branch had its connection on the south (Poland) end. The spur was north of the mainline and near the mouth of Eugenie Gulch. The task of loading and unloading shipments was simplified when the railroad constructed a platform twelve by thirty-two feet at the spur. However, as often as not, Eugenie Spur was empty or held only a solitary car on its rail.

The most imposing sight from the spur was a tall trestle a short distance up the mainline toward Poland. The bridge spanned Eugenie Creek just as its waters cascaded into the namesake of the area, Big Bug Creek. The original trestle collapsed one afternoon when floodwaters rushing down Eugenie Gulch splintered its support timbers, and the

structure fell into the raging creek waters. Travel over the branch line was halted while the bridge was strengthened and rebuilt. A credit to the engineers that designed it, the men that built it, and the section workers that maintained it, the new structure withstood everything that came at it and outlived the rest of the branch line by several years.

The area around Eugenie Spur is better known for romantic stories involving the railroad than for any ore that the area produced. Patrons of modern "saloons," antique stores, and park benches often recount stories of a sparkling new locomotive jumping the tracks near Eugenie and crashing down the hillside to the rocks below. As the tales generally go, the locomotive cannot be brought out of the ravine and still rests there amid the rocks and weeds with its brass gauges and much of its equipment intact. This is great stuff, the kind of story that makes campfires and "Western" magazines interesting, but is not factual.

In the latter days of the Poland Branch Line, locomotives "doubled up;" in case one derailed, the other was used to get it back on the rail. This technique was used several times, but derailments were generally minor. A derailment as described in the last paragraph never occurred. Even if it had, parts for the locomotives were always in short supply, very expensive, and salvaged from all damaged equipment down to the last bolt. Operation of the Poland Branch Line is rich in colorful history even without the embellishments of folklorists and "storytellers."

Eugenie Spur was removed with the mainline back to Henrietta Spur in November 1932, and little can be seen at the site. A portion of the old railroad

S.F., P. & P. Ry. locomotive No. 6 lays on her side after she jumped the tracks and overturned in Granite Dells a short distance from P. & E. Junction. The locomotive was repaired and back in service in a brief time. *Courtesy Sharlot Hall Museum.*

grade can be seen just off the dirt road near Eugenie Gulch, but the loading platform and mining activity left the area, not necessarily in that order, more than fifty years ago. The auto road cuts into the hillside and travels around the site of the old trestle, but wood debris and remnants of the pilings still rest in the canyon below. With thoughts of yesteryear and a look at the canyon, the trestle site is still very imposing.

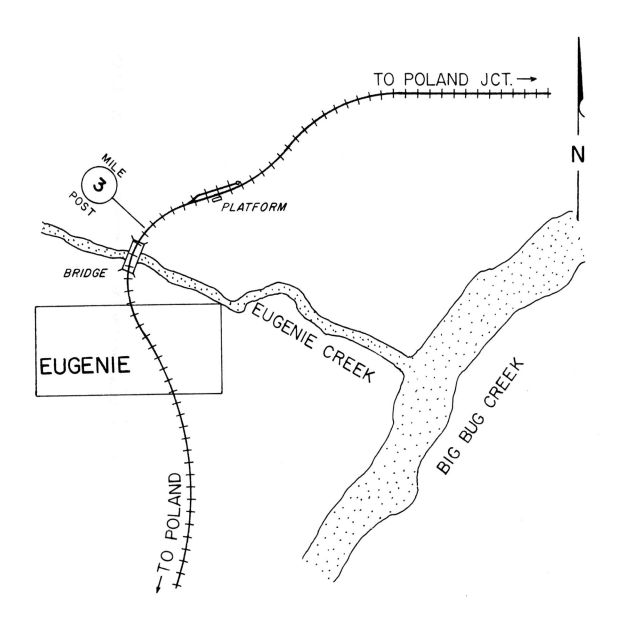

TO POLAND JCT. →

N

MILE POST
③

PLATFORM

BRIDGE

EUGENIE

EUGENIE CREEK

BIG BUG CREEK

TO POLAND

EUGENIE SPUR

SCALE: 1"= 600 FEET

MAP BY ROB KROHN

Smoke whorls behind the westbound locomotive as it rumbles noisily toward the little Providence depot. The terrain becomes rugged, timbered, and inspiring. The sound of the locomotive whistle joins the pounding of stamp mills and the clattering of mining machinery echoing from the hillsides.

PROVIDENCE STATION

1902 - 1932

The Bradshaw Mountain Railway Construction Company was formed in February 1901. The preliminary surveys were quickly completed, right-of-way obtained, and grading begun on the Poland Branch of this railway. The westward progress of the rail from Poland Junction through Providence and on to Poland was slowed by a variety of factors: an unusually harsh winter, a labor strike, and bedlam created by "gold fever." The latter malady resulted when gold was discovered while making a cut for the roadbed. The B.M. Ry. finally reached Providence on 7 April 1902, and whiskey and wine flowed freely during the celebration that ensued.

Providence was almost five miles west of Poland Junction. The town developed along Big Bug Creek and, during the community's early days, was often referred to as Big Bug. Providence should not be confused, as it often is, with the Big Bug Post Office and camp below the Big Bug (Henrietta) Mine or with the Big Bug Stage Station downstream on Big Bug Creek, which after 1881 was known as Mayer. The town of Providence was three miles west of the Boggs' cabin on the rocky wagon road just above the creek.

The swift mountain streams in the upper Big Bug area cut and eroded the terrain that lay before them. The cascading water carried the music and golden glitter of the high country. As the streams left the steep mountain slopes and joined Big Bug Creek, their waters slowed considerably. Settling to the bottom of the slower moving waters were debris and mineral deposits carried from upstream. These mineral deposits included gold dust, flakes, and nuggets. Mining for this type of deposit was called placering or placer mining. Methods varied from rudimentary gold "panning" to the use of sluices and elaborate dredges designed to separate the gold from debris. Unlike hardrock mining, which required considerable investment, placer mining took little more than a strong lower back and unending optimism. It was this type of mining that originally drew prospectors to Big Bug Creek near where Providence developed.

The upper Big Bug was first prospected by Boggs in 1863. Increasing numbers of miners searched the area for minerals in the 1870s and 1880s after hostilities with local Indians cooled. Placer claims and sluice boxes lined the creek, and lode claims dotted the hillsides as the 1880s brought Eastern capital and large mining companies into the area. The community inherited the name Providence from the Providence Gold Mining Company, which operated a mine near the townsite in 1899. Providence was surrounded by many producing mines of which the Oriental, Annie, Red Rock, Mammouth, Belcher, and Fortuna were the most notable. Although placer discoveries were still occasionally made in the 1890s, hardrock mining had rapidly become the important industry around Providence.

Providence began to take shape in the mid-1890s as miners constructed numerous small cabins and buildings along upper Big Bug Creek. A small business sector developed, and around it grew the town from which mining supplies, general provisions, and news were distributed to the nearby mines and camps. The arrival of the P. & E. in Mayer in 1898 caused a great amount of activity around Providence. There were already rumors that a branch railroad would be built from Huron along Big Bug Creek to the rough country near the Poland Mine. As the "Big Bug Railroad" reached the planning stages, the upper Big Bug area witnessed frenzied claim, mining, and other speculative maneuvering. The business sector at Providence grew to accommodate the needs of the rapidly increasing local population.

In January 1898, Providence supported two general merchandise stores, two barbershops, and four saloons. These firms, and their proprietors, enjoyed great local popularity. Frank Bliss manned the anvil in his blacksmith shop. He was the first businessman to hang his shingle in Providence, doing so in 1893. The business sector prospered and grew, enjoying its greatest years between 1899 and 1902 when the local mines were all being worked, having been developed to full capacity. The general store of Ed Trenberth was one of the most prosperous shops in town. Another popular store in 1902 was that of G. R. Sias and Frank Lecklider. This firm operated a branch store near the Poland Mine as well; both stores carried a large stock of hay and grain, mining supplies, groceries, and wearing apparel. They also conducted a lucrative general freighting business between the railroad siding at Providence and the Big Bug mines.

Other businesses which enjoyed continued success were those of B. F. Vasser and Frank Bliss. Vassar's barbershop proved so successful that he constructed a large new building in 1902. His establishment was "first class," featuring baths in porcelain tubs, exposed plumbing, and all the latest improvements. "Old timer" Frank Bliss' blacksmith shop also served as a rendezvous point where miners from all over the Bradshaw Mountains gathered to discuss the latest mining discovery and swap tall tales.

The community enjoyed great investment in local mines at the turn of the century. The Red Rock Mine was owned and operated by the United Verde Extension Mining Company of Jerome fame. The Lottie and Annie Mines were rapidly developed, and each had a ten-stamp mill clattering as it processed ore. Numerous other mines including the Mammouth, Great Belcher, Postmaster, and Oriental produced high quality ore in the 1890s.

The future appeared rosy for Providence. The town was home for approximately three hundred people by 1902. In the general election of that year, nearly one hundred votes were recorded in the Providence Voting Precinct. Enrollment in the school district, which was created in 1897 with ten pupils, grew to twenty-five. The community had

two telephone systems, daily stage service, and would soon have the railroad on the outskirts of town. A post office, appropriately named Providence, was opened on 4 April 1899, and merchant Bradford M. Crawford was appointed postmaster. Although it was described as a "fourth class" post office, its presence added a sense of respectability and permanence to the little town.

Providence, unlike many of the communities along the tracks, was not a direct creation of the railroad. In fact, the town's busiest days were after the railroad construction plans were announced and before the line was completed. The anticipation of the railroad going through Providence increased mining, merchant, and construction activity. However, this activity was based on speculation and wishful thinking, not on trade volume. The railroad hoped that the mines near town would prosper and grow with decreased transportation costs.

The Poland Branch of the B.M. Ry. paralleled Big Bug Creek and cut through the hillside a few hundred yards above the town and just below the Red Rock Mill. A depot measuring twelve by forty-four feet and a nine-car siding were built to serve Providence and were given that name. A water tank was also constructed to supply water for the climb to Poland. Supply trains first arrived in April 1902, and regular train scheduling began on 11 May 1902 with service to Poland. Wells Fargo and Western Union entered Providence in 1903 and operated in conjunction with the railroad.

It was not coincidental that a siding and depot were established at Providence. N.K. Fairbank, one of Murphy's associates and an investor in the P. & E. and B.M. Railways, owned controlling interest in the Providence Gold Mine. The B.M. Ry., after extensive research, determined a siding and depot were badly needed at the location.

Like most of the small towns in the Bradshaw Mountains, Providence did not have a deputy sheriff or jailhouse. Law enforcement was handled by the Yavapai County Sheriff from Prescott or, in Providence's waning days, by the deputy sheriff at Poland. The town was not known as a particularly rough one, but wherever four saloons flourished arguments took place. Miners and merchants were notorious for their lack of skill with firearms. Several whiskey-induced shoot-outs resulted in neither party being hit, and the men often drank together by nightfall. One shooting death did occur in Providence, but cooler heads usually prevailed, and most disagreements were quickly resolved.

Water was abundant in both Big Bug Creek and in shallow hillside wells. The townspeople had many occasions to wish that it was less abundant

This minor derailment was on the mainline near the Providence Depot. The town was down in the gulch to the left of this photograph, which looks west. *Courtesy Sharlot Hall Museum.*

near their homes. Water from the spring melt of snow and severe rainstorms of summer did great damage. Wagons, mining equipment, buildings, railroad trestles, and bullion were among the property swept away by swirling floods. Residents spent many hours downstream, hoping to find items that had been carried away. Their efforts usually went unrewarded.

A small, but valuable, shipment of gold bullion was claimed by the creek on a cold, ugly morning late one spring. Boiling clouds and long gray rains battered the countryside mercilessly. The sharp edge of the wind pushed the downpour into the smallest of crevices as timber cracked and trees crashed before the watery onslaught. Thunder cracked overhead as the ore wagon started toward Prescott to meet shipping deadlines. The wagon and precious cargo were lost when the road beneath them gave way to the strong current of ravaging flood waters. Search parties found the body of the teamster, horse carcasses, and pieces of the wagon, but the strongbox was never located. Perhaps another rich discovery lies just below the surface in Big Bug country.

Recreation centered around the saloons and boardinghouses for the single men and around home for those who were married. Card playing, horseshoes, reading, hunting, and dancing were favorite pastimes with almost everyone. Musicians and storytellers also attracted and held audiences for hours. Providence had a busy lodge of United Moderns, a fraternal organization, which held regular meetings and planned social activities. Labor Day, Independence Day, and Christmas were celebrated with great enthusiasm in Providence as in all Bradshaw Mountain communities.

George W. Smalley, the mining editor of the *Arizona Republican* in the 1890s, celebrated the Christmas of 1898 in Providence. The following exerpt from his article on that visit helps to capture the feel of life in an Arizona mining town at the turn of the century.

There was excitement the entire length of the [Big Bug] creek as I rode into [Providence] camp last night. Miners were bringing families down the trails from their homes perched on the mountain....The miners were coming down from their homes to attend the festivities and the gulch rang out joyous echoes as the children rushed toward the schoolhouse yelling their ovation to Santa Claus....

The snow on the mountains, whistling of the wind in the pines and the cold made it seem like Christmas eve. All that was needed was Santa. As I rode into camp the kids thought I was he. I was not surprised my horse was mistaken for a reindeer; he pranced excitedly as the boys approached....

The corral man was finishing his night's work early but he kindly made room for my horse and directed me to a store where I might get a lunch of sardines and crackers. The store keeper's wife was a kind lady and made a pot of tea to go with the meal and take away the chill of the night ride over the mountains. As I sat down to eat there was a renewal of the ovation to Santa Claus outside and presently Deputy Sheriff Johns rode into camp. His great mustache was white with frost and snow clung to his spurs and boots....I asked him where he was going to sleep and he said that was the least of his troubles for he knew where there was a stack of hay. I found there was not a bed in camp that was not taken and I made up my mind to follow Johns to the haystack.

The big schoolhouse was filled with miners and their families and the work benches were crowded....[Excitement] broke out as some little fellow discovered a drum hidden in the branches of the big Christmas tree which took up a large portion of the room....

The tree was heavily laden with presents. There was something for everyone in camp. Some of the more popular ones received a dozen gifts.

Before the presents were distributed there was an entertainment participated in by the students under Miss Henshaw....After the tree was unloaded the floor was cleared for dancing. This pleasure was enjoyed by a large number until after midnight.

Unfortunately, as was often the case, the mines around Providence did not fulfill the expectations of their owners or the businessmen dependent upon their success. Shortly after the Poland Branch of the Bradshaw Mountain Railway arrived at its terminus in Poland, it became obvious to Providence's residents that Poland would be the hub of mining activity in the Big Bug area. The local residents knew it was time to move on. The sad reality was that the placer mines near Providence, with few exceptions, were worked out before the turn of the century, and the hardrock mines were past their most productive years. Eastern investment, fraudulently lured by promoter Henry B. Clifford, kept the Great Belcher and Mammouth Mines operating after the ore was gone, but the

handwriting was on the wall.

The scene for the exodus may inadvertently have been set by the town's foresighted merchants. Sias and Lecklider, who operated stores in both Providence and Poland, concentrated their efforts in Poland after 1902. Ed Trenberth quickly did the same. He closed his mercantile concern in Providence and established the South Poland Hotel near the railroad depot in Poland. The mines and construction activity around Poland created opportunities not just for merchants and miners but for woodcutters, carpenters, and other tradesmen as well.

The demise of Providence was swift. Most of the residents moved just up the tracks to Poland, while a few others sought their fortunes elsewhere. The town, which boasted nearly one hundred voters in the general election of 1902, had only four registered voters in 1904, and its voting precinct was abolished prior to the primaries of 1906. Only one merchant remained in Providence after 1904. The post office was discontinued 15 November 1904, and mail for the local residents went to the post office at Henrietta. The Providence School District remained open through 1906 under the instruction of the Harriet Thomas. Her $70 per year teaching job was eliminated with the school district in 1907 due to a lack of students.

Over the next few years, there were exaggerated reports of new discoveries, and tailings were reprocessed several times. The railroad siding at Providence was used intermittently by small mining companies that shipped ore to Humboldt's mill and smelter. The railroad rapidly fell into disuse and disrepair as the mines of the upper Big Bug area were closed or abandoned. The road along Big Bug Creek went to ruin, and by the early 1920s, the once-flourishing settlement of Providence was badly decayed and neglected. Many of the structures were dismantled and moved to Poland by their original owners, while others fell prey to the elements and vandals. The railroad started removing its rail from Poland back toward Poland Junction in the summer of 1932; it completed the removal of rail and buildings through Providence and back to Henrietta Spur in November of that year.

Today, the remnants of an apple orchard stand above the creek, and the depot grade can still be seen at Providence. Nothing remains of the original buildings. Summer cottages, "private property" signs, and barbed wire stand where the town once stood.

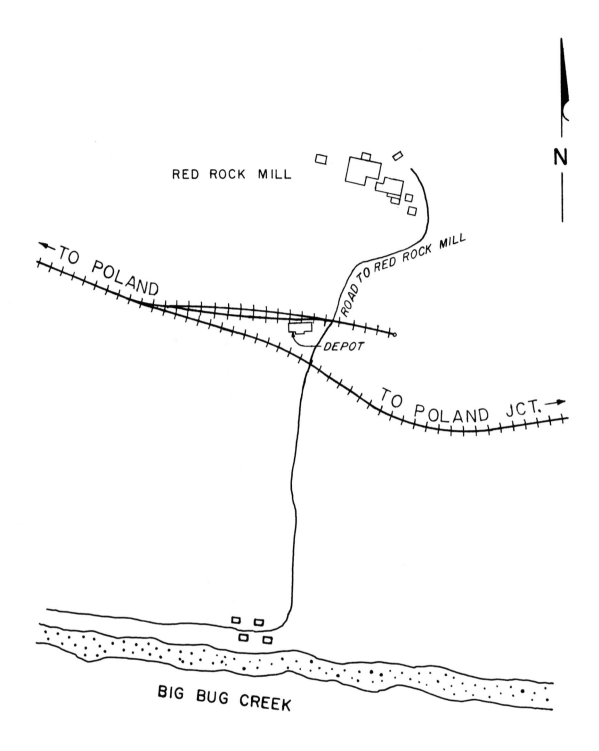

RED ROCK MILL

TO POLAND

ROAD TO RED ROCK MILL

DEPOT

TO POLAND JCT.

BIG BUG CREEK

N

PROVIDENCE STATION

SCALE: I"= 200 FEET

MAP BY ROB KROHN

As we travel through the only railroad tunnel on the Poland Branch, acrid, black smoke swirls through the open windows and makes our eyes water. We leave the tunnel none too soon and approach the last spur we will encounter before reaching Poland. Located one and one-half miles east of Poland, Block Spur is only a flagstop but is in beautiful country. The elevation at the spur is nearly six thousand feet, and the slow but steady climb from Providence has the locomotive breathing hard. The flag does not signal a stop, but we slow and wave to the men loading ore at the spur before continuing our climb to Poland.

BLOCK SPUR

1902 - 1932

There was only a handful of mines between Providence and Poland. The area was well-prospected, but mineral deposits in that particular area were few. The only real concentration of mining properties was midway between the two communities and a short distance from the rail.

Block Spur was named for Ed Block, the man who controlled the Merchant's Home Mine. Although other small mines clustered nearby, the Merchant's Home Mine was the largest producer in the immediate vicinity. Most of the mines produced silver and lead ore, but a couple of shallow copper deposits were also developed.

The railroad constructed a short spur in 1902 that served these mining properties. The spur was south of the mainline, had its connection on the south (Poland) end, and was capable of holding two cars. A loading platform was also built at the location and measured seven by twenty-two feet. No other structures were necessary, or were built, at the spur.

The Merchant's Home Mine produced silver ore that was high in lead content. More than 1,000 tons of crude ore were shipped from the Merchant's Home Mine during its years of activity, but the volume of production did not require any additional railroad construction at the spur. Production figures of the mine totaled nearly $70,000 before it was closed.

Today, the old railroad tunnel east of Block Spur is in surprisingly good condition and serves as a

Locomotive No. 5 of the S.F., P. & P. Ry. emerges from the tunnel on the branch line to Poland. *Courtesy Sharlot Hall Museum.*

silent tribute to Murphy and his railroad builders. The current road to Poland circumvents the tunnel, but many people stop to admire the wonderful piece of railroad construction. The site of Block Spur is difficult to locate, and only part of the old grade remains.

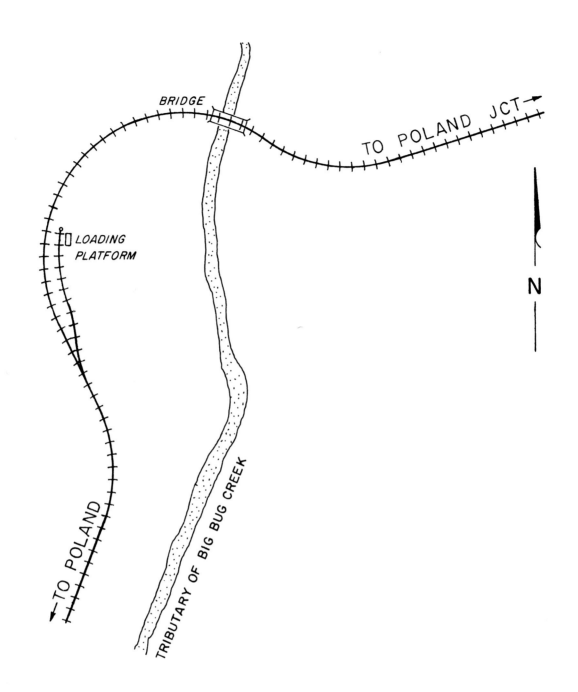

BRIDGE

TO POLAND JCT

N

LOADING
PLATFORM

TRIBUTARY OF BIG BUG CREEK

TO POLAND

BLOCK SPUR

SCALE: 1" = 200 FEET

MAP BY ROB KROHN

Our special excursion train over the old Prescott and Eastern and the Bradshaw Mountain Railway is nearing its final stop at the Poland depot. The sun slips behind the mountainous horizon, and the sky is painted brilliant orange. Long shadows dance on the tracks as we slowly cross Big Bug Creek and approach the depot. Light from within the depot casts an eerie glow as it cuts through the six-pane windows of the wooden building. Inside, the wife of the station agent sits patiently while her husband concludes his day's duties.

POLAND STATION

1902 - 1932

The mine, creek, and canyon at Poland were named for one of the pioneers of Big Bug country, Davis Robert Poland. He arrived in the area in 1864 and, along with his prospecting partners, Theodore W. Boggs and John M. Roberts, discovered several mineral deposits in the upper canyons of the Bradshaw Mountains. Many of Poland's discoveries were in the beautiful ravines near the headwaters of Big Bug Creek. Poland especially loved the heavily-wooded canyon that bore his name. He built a cabin in the canyon near the Poland Mine and lived there until his death in 1882.

Although there were flurries of activity at the Poland Mine in 1887 and again in the mid-90s, the community of Poland was a creation of the railroad. In 1900, Frank M. Murphy and associates obtained the Poland Mine and established the Poland Mining Company to develop the property. Several of the officers of this company were on the Board of Directors of the Santa Fe, Prescott and Phoenix Railway and the Prescott and Eastern Railway companies. It was not surprising that the survey for the branch railroad up Big Bug Creek brought the rail to the mine's doorstep.

The survey of the branch line from Poland Junction to the Poland Mine was completed in early 1901. Private dwellings and business enterprises sprang up quickly near the Poland Mine along the surveyed right-of-way. Poland Canyon, while picturesque and attractive, was also narrow, rocky, and steep. Houses were under construction on the hillsides as crews leveled clearings in the canyon for

building sites and graded the roadbed. Construction of the townsite continued well into the summer of 1902, although the rail reached Poland in late April and the first regularly scheduled run was made early the next month. Even as the first train rolled into the community, thirty-eight men were employed constructing electrical and water systems.

The town started to take shape in late 1901. Many of the merchants from Providence purchased property in Poland Canyon, established their businesses there, and awaited completion of the railroad. A post office was granted to the young town on 16 November 1901. The first postmaster, merchant James Sias, served in the position for only two months before turning the responsibility over to his business partner, Frank Lecklider. Sias and Lecklider, formerly of Providence, were among the first merchants established in Poland and operated the post office out of the corner of their general merchandise store.

Among the other merchants who established themselves early in Poland was the Trenberth family, also formerly of Providence. The Trenberths built the South Poland Hotel, a restaurant, and a saloon a short distance from the Poland depot. Hungry and weary travelers enjoyed the comforts and hospitality of the hotel for several years. There were complaints about the around-the-clock clanging of the Poland Mill. The noise echoed through the canyon and kept visitors awake all night. However, the local residents and regular

This trestle on the Poland Branch of the Bradshaw Mountain Railway crossed Big Bug Creek. *Courtesy Sharlot Hall Museum.*

In this 1907 photograph of Poland, the railway depot, turntable, mill, and Poland-Walker Tunnel are visible. *Courtesy Sharlot Hall Museum.*

A short distance from the depot, the South Poland Hotel offered fine food, drink, and lodging to hungry and weary travelers to Poland. Ed Trenberth, the hotel's personable proprietor, is clad in the white apron. *Courtesy Sharlot Hall Museum.*

The old and "new" form of transportation are contrasted in this photograph as a pack train of burros crosses Big Bug Creek just to the left of the railroad turntable in Poland. One of the town's boardinghouses is seen in the background. *Courtesy Arizona Department of Library, Archives and Public Records.*

The station agent poses on the platform in front of the small Poland Depot. *Courtesy Arizona Department of Library, Archives and Public Records.*

visitors grew accustomed to the noise, awakening if the mill shut down during the night.

Although there were private homes and buildings scattered through Poland Canyon, the townsite was dominated by the structures of the Bradshaw Mountain Railway. Railroad activity centered around the depot and the turntable. The depot itself was not a large structure, measuring only twelve by thirty-three feet, but around it was built a long platform. Cut into the hillside just below the depot was the turntable. It allowed locomotives to turn around before heading down the track on their way back to Prescott. Other railroad structures in town included a residence built for the station agent, coal bins, tool houses, and other houses for maintenance personnel.

The railroad constructed five separate spurs in Poland. The mainline was cut along the southern wall of the canyon, and the spurs were all graded to the north of the right-of-way. The spur connections were on the west end of the line to allow the locomotives to gain enough speed to climb the steep spurs. The first spur encountered was the Poland Mill Spur. It was 510 feet long and ran to the loading bins of the Poland Mill just below the mine. The Turntable Spur was the second one to leave the mainline. Only 264 feet long, this spur was nearly parallel to the mainline and terminated at the concrete and steel turntable. The turntable was over sixty-four feet across and nearly five feet thick, not including the concrete foundation. The third and fourth spurs converged in front of the depot. This allowed the engineer to pull the cars in his train onto either spur, uncouple them, turn his locomotive around on the turntable, and then recouple the rolling stock that was headed back down the mountain. Locomotives always led the trains into and out of Poland. The last spur in Poland was in front of the South Poland Hotel and served the Poland Extension Mine and other local mines. A warehouse, coal bins, and ore bins were built and maintained by various mining companies along this spur.

Relatively few railroad mishaps occurred at

The "lucky seven spot" of the S.F., P. & P. Ry. is seen steaming toward the Poland Depot. *Courtesy Sharlot Hall Museum.*

This view from the Poland Depot looks past the turntable and toward the mainline to Prescott. P. & E. locomotive No. 12 leaves a trail of smoke as she rumbles down the rail from Poland. *Courtesy Sharlot Hall Museum.*

S.F., P. & P. Ry. engine No. 9 is shown on the Poland Turntable. *Courtesy Sharlot Hall Museum.*

Poland, but those that did often involved the turntable. One such incident took place in early October 1903 when the "lucky seven spot" locomotive (engine No. 7) was backing onto the turntable. The hind wheels of the tender jumped the tracks and wedged against the rail. Some chopping, cutting, cussing, and plenty of elbow grease succeeded in getting the wheels back on the track and the engine back in operation. Most accidents caused minor delays in operation and were not life or equipment threatening.

The Poland Mine was on the slope only a few hundred feet above the townsite. The gold vein was worked by a tunnel gouged eight hundred feet into the mountain, and the ore was processed by a twenty-stamp mill between the mine and the railroad spur. In 1901, Murphy and his associates decided to extend the tunnel completely through the mountain. Outwardly, the men hoped new ore deposits would be discovered by the ambitious tunnel project, but there were other motives behind the construction of the tunnel. Several

mines on the other side of the mountain near Lynx Creek produced considerable amounts of ore in 1900 and sought to cut their ore shipping costs. Not surprisingly, another of Frank Murphy's companies, the Development Company of America, owned and operated the Lynx Creek mines. The Poland Tunnel, which was also called the Poland-Lynx Creek Tunnel and the Poland-Walker Tunnel, was driven 8,017 feet through the mountain and allowed Lynx Creek mines to ship ore directly through the mountain to the Poland Mill. After the ore was processed, it traveled the railroad to the Humboldt smelter.

The Poland Tunnel was completed in May 1904 at a cost of $500,000. It was driven from both sides of the mountain and was cut so accurately that when both tunnels met they were only six inches off center. The work was difficult, progressing at a rate of only two hundred feet a month from each end. Most of the tunnel was constructed with a one percent grade sloped toward Poland, but the end farthest from the community was driven at a three

136

The Poland-Walker Tunnel was off-limits to everyone except mining company employees. These guards appear serious about enforcing the "No Admittance" signs. *Courtesy Arizona Department of Library, Archives and Public Records.*

This photograph shows the inside of the Poland-Walker Tunnel shortly after its completion. Notice that this portion of the tunnel was through hard rock and required little or no timbering. *Courtesy Arizona Department of Library, Archives and Public Records.*

This view of the Poland Mining Company office was taken circa 1914. Note the large waste pile below the Poland-Walker Tunnel. *Courtesy Arizona Historical Foundation, Hayden Library, Arizona State University.*

percent grade. The downgrade toward Poland not only helped move the ore in that direction but also allowed water for use in the mill to be piped by gravity.

Discoveries of gold and silver were made during the construction of the tunnel, and activity in and around it was hectic. Originally the tunnel was ten feet wide and eight feet high. The ore was transported in iron cars pulled by mules. The tunnel was enlarged in 1905, and donkeys and gasoline engines provided the power to move the ore. In 1907, a 30 inch gauge railroad was completed through the tunnel, but this venture was more promotional than practical. The little railroad was short-lived; soon after it was completed, the Lynx Creek mines shut down for several years.

The community below the Poland Mine grew and prospered from all the mining and railroad activity. Production increased to $130,000 in 1907 while the population of the town grew to almost eight hundred people. Shipments of ore over the railroad were extremely heavy, and Poland was the center of activity in Big Bug country.

The first few years after the railroad reached Poland the depot was a busy place. The Poland Branch Line was completed in 1902, and the Bradshaw Mountain Railway stationed a locomotive in its yard at Poland. The engine pulled ore cars from spurs in Poland to the siding at Poland Junction in the morning and made another run back in the afternoon. Although in many locations a single agent represented Wells Fargo, Western Union, and the railroad, the heavy shipping volume at Poland required a separate agent to handle the Wells Fargo transactions. The depot was a bustling place filled with news and financiers from the East, promoters and mining men from the West, and golden ore from the earth beneath.

High in the Bradshaw Mountains, the depot platform was often covered with snow, and the six-pane windows chilled with frost during the winter months. The modest Poland depot was warmed by a potbelly stove and the smile of the railroad agent assigned there. He not only sold tickets and shared good cheer but also processed and recorded waybills, train register checks, and running orders.

From his desk, which was usually piled high with paperwork, the agent had an unobstructed view of the turntable, the mainline from Providence, and the mainline tail just to the west. The telegraph key was near the desk and clattered away as agents along the line sent and received telegrams. Beyond the ticket window was the passenger waiting room lined with long wooden benches and the baggage room filled with freight. The depot did not have a modern restroom, but a two-seat "privy" stood a short distance away. The Poland depot, painted the standard colonial yellow of the Santa Fe System, was simple but functional in design, and was the shipping point for thousands of dollars of ore.

From its modest beginnings in 1901, the town became one of the most modern in Central Arizona. It offered the conveniences of electricity, telephones, and a water system and was proud of its county jailhouse finished in 1903. A constable maintained law and order the best he could in a town that heartily supported six saloons. Shots were fired occasionally, but more often the constable stopped fistfights, dried out drunks, and patrolled the community.

In addition to the jailhouse, other municipal improvements were established in Poland. A schoolhouse was built in 1902 and was attended by twenty-two students in that year. It was expanded, and forty-four students sat on the hardwood benches to study the three "r's" in 1908. On Sunday the schoolhouse doubled as a church. Sunday school and the sermon were taught from the teacher's desk. A small hospital was operated in town by Dr. R.T. Rolph. Like all early doctors, Dr. Rolph made house calls and thus spent much of his time on the road in his buggy. He traveled to any nearby camp where someone was sick or injured but maintained his clinic in Poland.

Numerous businesses were represented in town. Several mining companies had offices there, including the Poland Mining Company. As mentioned, Wells Fargo and Western Union established offices in the railroad depot in 1903 and operated there for several years. Several saloons, boardinghouses, the general merchandise store, hotel, and post office were quite popular in the community.

The Poland Mining Company constructed numerous buildings. Its office stood a few feet away from the railroad depot. The other buildings of the mining company were the boardinghouse, two bunkhouses, machine shop, boiler house, two storehouses, stable, blacksmith shop, assay office, water tanks, and twenty miners' cabins.

The residents of Poland respected their community and were very active politically. By 1904, eighty-six men were registered to vote in town, and the elections were hotly contested. The Republicans met in the schoolhouse to vote in the primaries while the Democrats gathered in the Lecklider boardinghouse and cast their ballots. The schoolhouse was the polling place for the general elections.

The political activism of the local miners reached its peak in 1903 when they went on strike for shorter work shifts. The Western Federation of Miners Union was strong in Poland, as it was in McCabe, Crown King, along Lynx Creek, and elsewhere in the county. The union fought for and won a reduction of the work day from ten to eight hours without any reduction in pay. Injunctions were granted both sides, and legal maneuvering delayed a final judgment for several months. Compromise, the economic panic of 1907, and abandonment of mines eventually weakened the union in Poland, but the men continued to make their feelings known at the polls.

Mining activity at Poland slowed after 1907. The national economic recession of that year depressed the metals market, and most mines closed down. The Poland Tunnel shut down in 1907 and remained closed until 1916. The Poland Mine was still operated, although production decreased as the vein "played out." The mine remained open until 1912, when it was considered to be exhausted by the Poland Mining Company. The Poland Mill stayed in operation through 1913 as it reprocessed tailings and waste material. The total production of the Poland Mine was estimated as $750,000, and the production of small mines nearby combined to equal that figure.

When mining was curtailed near Poland, the community suffered. Enrollment in the local school decreased and forced the school to close as parents left town in search of work. Wells Fargo closed its office, as did the mining companies. With each month that passed, the community became quieter and smaller. In 1912, only sixteen votes were cast in the general election at Poland. Within three months of the election, the post office in Poland was discontinued on 15 February 1913.

The community did not experience the resurgence from World War I that so many other communities enjoyed. Small amounts of ore were mined near Poland in 1914 and 1916, but the amount of ore shipped was minimal. The Poland Tunnel was reopened in 1916, and shipments were made through it from the Lynx Creek mines. Shipments continued through 1920 when the tunnel was again closed for several years.

The little life that remained in the Big Bug country left. Scheduled railroad service was discontinued on the Poland Branch in 1920. The railroad fell into disrepair as its ties and buildings rotted from neglect. Weeds grew between the rails, and paint peeled from the walls of the weathered little depot. In Poland, vacant and decayed buildings lined the canyon. Rock walls crumbled, mine tunnels caved-in, and only silence echoed through the canyon.

The railroad line to Poland was reconditioned in the late twenties as production resumed from Lynx Creek mines, but had little effect on the near ghost town. Occasionally a small deposit of lead or zinc was discovered, but ore shipments over the once busy railroad were pitifully infrequent. The Santa Fe Railway abandoned its track to Poland in the summer of 1932 and completed the removal and salvaging of its property in the community in November of that year.

The old railroad roadbed to Poland was used as an automobile road into the area. As with the abandoned roadbed to Crown King, the trestles were planked over in order to be used by automobiles. Eventually, the road was cut into the hillside and detoured the old bridges. Traffic to the community consisted primarily of mining men who sampled the canyon for mineral deposits and rodents that picked through twenty years of broken dreams.

Poland Canyon did not witness much activity again until the 1940s. A twentieth century entrepreneur bought the exhausted mining claims in the canyon, subdivided them into lots for summer cottages, and renamed the community Breezy Pines. The idea was enthusiastically received, and summer houses soon occupied the former townsite of Poland.

Today, Poland Canyon remains one of the most picturesque locations in Arizona. Big Bug Creek still trickles though the canyon, and a cool breeze whistles through the tall pines. The old buildings have all disappeared, but the rock foundations of the Poland Mill and a portion of the concrete base of the railroad turntable still remain. Above the mill foundation, the Poland Tunnel is caved-in, but a U.S. Forest Service sign marks the site and gives a brief history. Sunlight filters through the pines and warms the air; memories of the past filter through the mind and warm the soul. Poland, once the pride of upper Big Bug country, has faded into yesteryear but is not forgotten.

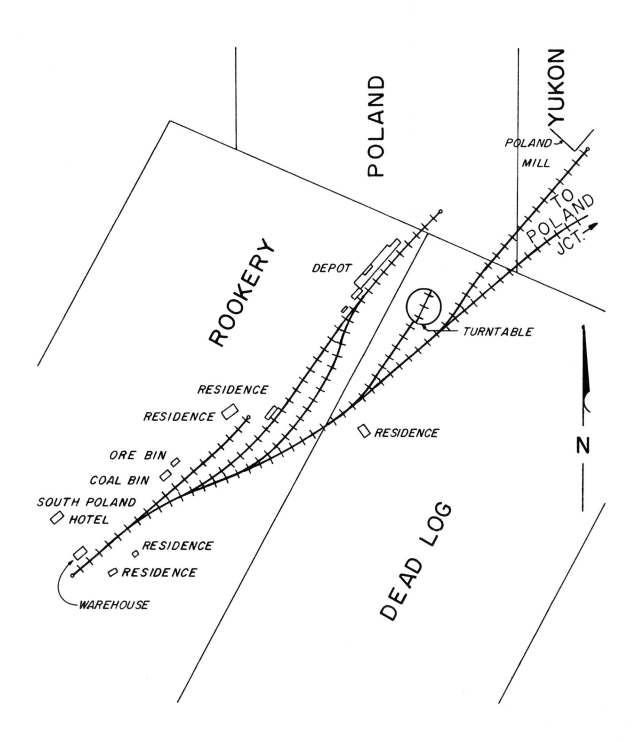

POLAND

YUKON

POLAND MILL

TO POLAND JCT.

ROOKERY

DEPOT

TURNTABLE

RESIDENCE

RESIDENCE

RESIDENCE

N

ORE BIN

COAL BIN

SOUTH POLAND

HOTEL

DEAD LOG

RESIDENCE

RESIDENCE

WAREHOUSE

POLAND STATION

SCALE: 1" = 200 FEET

MAP BY ROB KROHN

EPILOGUE

The locomotive has a full head of steam and journeys down the rail toward Prescott. The long, mournful sound of the steam whistle breaks the night air and signals the end of an era. We stand on the depot platform and watch as first the train and then its black trail of smoke fade from view and into the past. The popular boardinghouses and restaurants, heavily patronized saloons, and family mercantile establishments pale in the evening darkness. Silence fills the countryside, and in vivid contrast to the great excitement and activity of yesteryear, the community sleeps quietly.

The railroad and many of the communities it served have left the mountains. They only exist on antiquated maps, in brittle scrapbooks of pioneer families, and in week-overgrown cemeteries. Although each spring brings life anew to the Bradshaw Range in the form of green mountain grass and colorful wild flowers, the sun glinting on crumbled foundations, rotted railroad ties, and rusted hardware reminds one of the past. Flagstone quarries, leaching ponds, and silence occupy the present. Perhaps the ghosts of miners and railroaders know what the Bradshaw Mountains hold for the future. A flurry of breeze seems to bid us farewell as we leave the still-rugged countryside.

This classification lamp saw many years of service on the locomotives of the old S.F., P. & P. Ry. A pair of these lamps was displayed on the front of each steam locomotive and indicated its running classification. *Sayre Collection.*

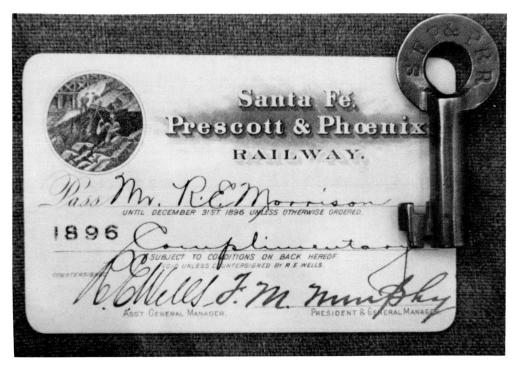

Santa Fe, Prescott and Phoenix Railway pass and switch key. *Sayre Collection.*

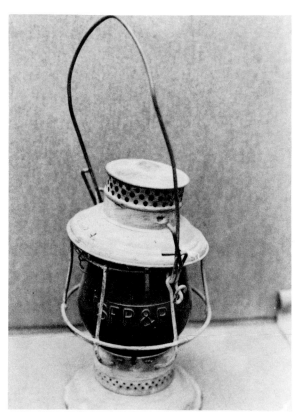

This hand lantern, its green globe embossed with the initials of the Pea Vine, was used for many years on the Bradshaw Mountain Railway. *Sayre Collection.*

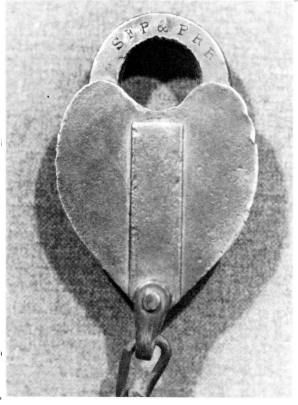

This switch lock, wearing the initials of the Santa Fe, Prescott and Phoenix Railway, hung on a switch-stand alongside the shiny steel rail of the P. & E. Ry. and, for many years, helped direct traffic on that scenic railroad. *Sayre Collection; photograph by author.*

143

BIBLIOGRAPHY

Manuscript Sources

Arizona Corporation Commission. Phoenix, Arizona.
Articles of incorporation.

Arizona Department of Mineral Resources. Phoenix, Arizona.
Various mine files.

Arizona Public Service Company Archives. Phoenix, Arizona.
Arizona Public Service Company shelf index.

Atchison, Topeka and Santa Fe Railway Company. Winslow, Arizona.
Right-of-way maps.
Station plat maps.

Sharlot Hall Museum. Prescott, Arizona.
Various mine files.
Photographic collections.

Special Collections. Northern Arizona University. Flagstaff, Arizona.
Dunning, Charles H., Collection.
Perrin, Edward Burt, Collection.

United States Department of Land Management. Phoenix, Arizona.
General Land Office plat maps.
Original field notes.

Yavapai County Courthouse. Prescott, Arizona.
Assessor's Office.
Residential property record card file.
Clerk of the Court's Office.
United States District Court Cases.
Recorder's Office.
Books of articles of incorporation.
Books of deeds.
Books of mines.

Personal Interviews

The author interviewed more than forty pioneer Arizonans when writing this manuscript. Their contributions to and assistance in this project were substantial. Sadly, oral history remains a largely untapped, and shrinking, source of knowledge and information.

Unpublished Theses

Anderson, Lucille. "Railroad Transportation Through Prescott." MA thesis, University of Arizona, 1934.

Byrkit, James Ward. "Life and Labor in Arizona, 1901-1921: with Particular Reference to the Deportations of 1917." Ph.D. dissertation, Claremont Graduate College, 1972.

Henderson, Patrick C. "A Short History of the Prescott Bradshaw Mining Districts." MA thesis, University of Arizona, 1958.

Pearson, Mary S. "Edward Burt Perrin, 1839-1932; A Southern Entrepreneur in the American West." MA thesis, Northern Arizona University, 1968.

Sayre, John W. "Mines, Men, and Machinery: A Study of Copper Mining in the Bradshaw Mountains 1875-1979." MA thesis, Northern Arizona University, 1979.

Smith, Jimmy Harold. "Prostitution in Arizona Mining Camps, 1870-1917." MA thesis, Northern Arizona University, 1977.

Spude, Robert Lester. "The Mineral Frontier in Transition: Arizona Copper Mining 1880-1885." MA thesis, Arizona State University, 1976.

Newspapers and Periodicals

Arizona Citizen [Tucson].
Arizona Journal-Miner [Prescott].
Arizona Mining Journal [Tucson].
Arizona Republican [Phoenix].
Arizona Republic [Phoenix].

Big Bug Copper News [Mayer].
Engineering and Mining Journal [New York].
Mining and Scientific Press [San Francisco].
Phoenix Herald
Pick and Drill [Prescott].
Prescott Courier
Prescott Weekly Courier
Prospect [Prescott].
Tempe News
Weekly Reflex [Mayer].
Yavapai Magazine [Prescott].

Government Documents

Elsing, Morris J. and Robert E. S. Heineman. "Arizona Metal Production," Arizona Bureau of Mines, Economic Series No. 19, Bulletin No. 140. Tucson: University of Arizona Press, 1936.

Lindgren, Waldemar. *Ore Deposits of the Jerome and Bradshaw Mountains Quadrangles, Arizona*. Washington: Government Printing Office, 1926.

Raymond, Rossiter. *Statistics of Mines and Mining in the States and Territories West of the Rocky Mountains*. Washington: Government Printing Office, 1870.

United States Bureau of Mines. "Aerial Tramways for Metal Mines," Part I. Information Circular No. 6948. Washington: Government Printing Office, 1937.

United States Bureau of the Census. Twelfth Decennial Census of the United States, manuscript returns for Yavapai County, Territory of Arizona.

United States Department of Agriculture. Map of the Prescott National Forest, 1970. Scale: one-half inch equals one mile.

United States Department of Commerce. *Historical Statistics of the United States: Colonial Times to 1970, Part I.* Washington: Government Printing Office, 1975.

———. *Mineral Resources of the United States: Calendar Year 1925.* Washington: Government Printing Office, 1928.

———. *Mineral Resources of the United States: Calendar Year 1930.* Washington: Government Printing Office, 1933.

United States Department of Interior. *Mineral Resources of the United States: Calendar Year 1905.* Washington: Government Printing Office, 1906.

———. *Mineral Resources of the United States: Calendar Year 1918.* Washington: Government Printing Office, 1919.

———. *Mineral Resources of the United States: Calendar Year 1922.* Washington: Government Printing Office, 1923.

Wilson, Eldred D., J.B. Cunningham, and G.M. Butler. "Arizona Lode Gold Mines and Gold Mining." Arizona Bureau of Mines, Mineral Technology Series No. 37, Bull. No. 137. Tucson: University of Arizona Press, 1934.

Books

Alexander, William. *The Sixty-Five Years of Arizona Post Office History Since Statehood.* In press.

Bancroft, Hubert Howe. *History of Arizona and New Mexico: 1530-1888.* San Francisco: The History Publishers Company, 1889,

Bryant, Keith L., Jr. *History of the Atchison, Topeka and Santa Fe Railway.* Lincoln, Nebraska: University of Nebraska Press, 1982.

Byrkit, James W., *Forging the Copper Collar: Arizona's Labor Management War 1901-1921.* Tucson: University of Arizona Press, 1982.

Chappel, Gordon S. *Rails to Carry Copper.* Boulder, Colorado: Pruett Publishing Company, 1975.

Cleland, Robert Glass. *A History of Phelps-Dodge 1834-1950.* New York: Knopf Publishing Company, 1952.

Dunning, Charles H. and Edward H. Peplow, Jr. *Rock to Riches: The Story of American Mining...Past, Present, and Future as Reflected in the Colorful History of Mining in Arizona.* Phoenix: Southwest Publishing Company, 1959.

Dutton, Allen A. and Diane Bunting. *Arizona: Then and Now.* Phoenix: Privately Published, 1981.

Ferris, Robert G., ed. *The American West: An Appraisal.* Santa Fe: Museum of New Mexico Press, 1963.

Fleming, Lawrence J. *Ride a Mile and Smile the While: A History of the Phoenix Street Railway 1887-1948.* Phoenix: Swaine Publishers, 1977.

Florin, Lambert, *Ghost Towns of the West.* Seattle: Superior Publishing Company, 1970.

Granger, Byrd H. *Arizona Place Names.* Tucson: University of Arizona Press, 1970.

Greever, William. *Bonanza West: The Story of the Western Mining Rushes, 1848-1900.* Norman: University of Oklahoma Press, 1963

Hinton, Richard J. *1000 Old Arizona Mines.* Toyahville, Texas: Frontier Book Company, 1962.

Hodge, Hiram C. *1877: Arizona as it Was.* Chicago: Rio Grande Press, 1965.

Jackson, W. Turrentine. *Treasure Hill: Portrait of a Silver Mining Camp.* Tucson: University of Arizona Press, 1963.

Jensen, Vernon H. *Heritage of Conflict: Labor Relations in the Nonferrous Metals Industry up to 1930.* Ithaca, New York: Cornell University Press, 1950.

Joralemon, Ira Beamon. *Copper: The Encompassing Story of Mankind's First Metal.* Berkeley: Howell-North Publishing Company, 1973.

Magma Copper Company. *The Plant.* San Manuel, Arizona: Newmont Mining Corporation, no date.

Marshall, James. *Santa Fe: The Railroad that Built an Empire.* New York: Random House, 1945.

McNally, Rand. *Pocket Map and Shipper's Guide to Arizona.* New York: Rand McNally and Company, 1910.

Morgan, Joseph H. *Summary of the Laws Regulating the Location, Holding, and Transfer of Mines and Mining Claims in Arizona.* Phoenix: McNeil Publishing Company, 1917.

Morgan, Learah Cooper, ed. *Echoes of the Past: Tales of Old Yavapai.* 2nd ed. Prescott, Arizona: Yavapai Cowbelles, 1955.

Murbarger, Nell. *Ghosts of the Adobe Walls.* Tucson: Treasure Chest Publishers, 1977.

Myrick, David F. *Pioneer Arizona Railroads.* Golden, Colorado: Colorado Railroad Museum.

———. *Railroads of Arizona, Vol. I.* San Diego: Howell-North, 1980.

———. *Railroads of Arizona, Vol. II.* San Diego: Howell-North, 1981.

Neale, Walter Garfield. *The Mines Handbook, XVII.* New York: Mines Handbook Company, 1926.

Paul, Rodman Wilson. *Mining Frontiers of the Far West, 1848-1880.* Albuquerque: University of New Mexico Press, 1963.

Petersen, Richard H. *The Bonanza Kings: The Social and Business Behavior of Western Mining Entrepreneurs, 1870-1900.* Lincoln: University of Nebraska Press, 1977.

Potter, Alvina. *The Many Lives of the Lynx.* Prescott: Privately Published, 1964.

Quebbeman, Frances E. *Medicine in Territorial Arizona.* Phoenix: Arizona Historical Foundation, 1966.

Raud, Lenox H. *The Mines Handbook, XV.* Suffern, New York: Mines Information Bureau, 1931.

Rickard, Thomas Arthur. *The History of American Mining.* New York: McGraw-Hill Publishing Company, 1932.

———. *The Romance of Mining.* New York: MacMillan Publishing Company, 1944.

Sherman, James E. and Barbara H. *Ghost Towns of Arizona.* Norman: University of Oklahoma Press, 1969.

Smith, Duane A. *Rocky Mountain Mining Camps: The Urban Frontier.* Bloomington: University of Indiana Press, 1967.

Spence, Clark C. *British Investments and the American Mining Frontier 1860-1901.* Ithaca, New York: Cornell University Press, 1958.

Spude, Robert Lester and Stanley W. Paher. *Central Arizona Ghost Towns.* Las Vegas: Nevada Publications, 1978.

Stevens, Horace J. *The Copper Handbook: A Manual of the Copper Industry of the World,* 10 volumes. Houghton, Michigan: the author, 1900-1912.

Stevens, Robert, ed. *Echoes of the Past: Tales of Old Yavapai. 2nd Vol.* Prescott, Arizona: Yavapai Cowbelles, 1964.

Theobald, John and Lillian. *Arizona Territory Post Offices and Postmasters.* Tempe, Arizona: Arizona Historical Foundation, 1961.

———. *Wells Fargo in Arizona Territory.* Tempe, Arizona: Arizona Historical Foundation, 1978.

Varney, Phillip. *Arizona's Best Ghost Towns.* Flagstaff: Northland Press, 1980.

Wahmann, Russell. *Auto Road Log...Follow the Narrow Gauge, Have Fun with History, Spectacular Scenery.* Jerome: Jerome Historical Society, 1982.

———. *Cleopatra's Railroads: Railroading in the Verde Valley.* Jerome: Jerome Community Service Organization, 1975.

Weed, Walter Harvey. *The Copper Handbook: A Manual of the Copper Industry of the World, XI.* Houghton, Michigan: Stevens Copper Handbook Company, 1914.

———. *The Copper Handbook: A Manual of the Copper Industry of the World, XII.* Houghton, Michigan: Stevens Copper Handbook Company, 1916.

Young, Herbert V. *Ghosts of Cleopatra Hill: Men and Legends of Old Jerome.* Jerome: Jerome Historical Society, 1964.

———. *They Came to Jerome: The Billion Dollar Copper Camp.* Jerome: Jerome Historical Society, 1972.

Young, Otis E., Jr. *The Mining Men.* Kansas City, Mo.: Lowell Press, 1974.

———. *Western Mining: An Informal Account of Precious Metals Prospecting, Placering, Lode Mining, and Milling on the American Frontier from Spanish Times to 1893.* Norman: University of Oklahoma Press, 1970.

Articles

Anderson, Lucille. "Railroad Transportation through Prescott: The Prescott and Arizona Central Railroad." *Arizona Historical Review,* Vol. 7, no. 3 (1936), pp. 55-72.

Dubofsky, Melvyn. "The Origins of Western Working Class Radicalism 1890-1905," *Labor History,* Spring 1966, pp. 131-154.

Greever, William S. "Railway Development in the Southwest." *New Mexico Historical Review,* Vol. 32, no. 2 (1957), pp. 151-203.

Henderson, Patrick C. "Bradshaw Bonanza." *New Mexico Historical Review,* April 1963, pp. 151-162.

Hinton, Harwood P. "Frontier Speculations: A Study of the Walker Mining Districts." *Pacific Historical Review,* August 1960, pp. 245-255.

Spence, Clark C. "British Investment and the American Mining Frontier, 1860-1914." *New Mexico Historical Review,* April 1961, pp. 121-137.

Spude, Robert Lester. "A Land of Sunshine and Silver: Silver Mining in Central Arizona 1871-1885." *Journal of Arizona History,* Spring 1975, pp. 29-76.

———. "Swansea, Arizona: The Fortunes and Misfortunes of a Copper Camp." *Journal of Arizona History,* Winter 1976, pp. 375-395.

———. "A Tour of the Big Bug Mining District." *Journal of Arizona History,* Winter 1972, pp. 253-274.

Thorpe, Winifred L. "Joe Mayer and His Town." *Journal of Arizona History,* Fall 1978, pp. 131-168.

Index